Christian Society and the Crusades

1198-1229

THE MIDDLE AGES SERIES

Ruth Mazo Karras, General Editor
Edward Peters, Founding Editor

A complete list of books in this series
is available from the publisher

Christian Society and the Crusades 1198-1229

Sources in Translation, including The Capture of Damietta *by Oliver of Paderborn translated with notes by* JOHN J. GAVIGAN

Edited, with an Introduction by EDWARD PETERS

PENN

UNIVERSITY OF PENNSYLVANIA PRESS/PHILADELPHIA

10 9 8 7 6 5 4

Published by
University of Pennsylvania Press
Philadelphia, Pennsylvania 19104-4011

Library of Congress Catalog Card Number: 78-163385
ISBN (paperback) 0-8122-1024-7
Printed in the United States of America on acid-free paper

Contents

Editor's Note

Several of the texts reprinted in this volume were originally issued in the University of Pennsylvania Series, *Translations and Reprints from the Original Sources of European History.* This series, which began in 1894 and continued intermittently until the 1950's, was the first major attempt to place scholarly translations of primary source materials for the study of history in the hands of students in an inexpensive paperback format, although the series appeared only in hardback after 1940. In reissuing several of these smaller works in comprehensive volumes with additional materials, the Editor and the University of Pennsylvania Press have been guided by a conviction that these works of translation are still useful to the student and general reader and that the addition of material not in the original series contributes to a more complete understanding of the periods, episodes, and themes involved.

Introduction

> Beasts of many kinds are attempting to destroy the vineyard of
> the Lord of Sabaoth, and their onset has so far succeeded
> against it that over no small area thorns have sprung up instead
> of vines and (with grief we report it!) the vines themselves are
> variously infected and diseased, and instead of the grape they
> bring forth the wild grape. Therefore we invoke the testimony
> of Him, who is a faithful witness in the Heavens, that of all the
> desires of our heart we long chiefly for two in this life, namely
> that we may work successfully to recover the Holy Land and
> to reform the Universal Church, both of which call for atten-
> tion so immediate as to preclude further apathy or delay unless
> at the risk of great and serious danger.[1]

Thus, in his letter of 1213 to the ecclesiastical officials of the
province of Canterbury, did Pope Innocent III (1198–1216)
depict the dangers to universal Christendom and the two
most pressing tasks before it. To be sure, the first fifteen years
of Innocent's pontificate had not neglected these problems,
and the great Pope had sent thousands of letters concerning
the threatened state of Christendom—letters which had
begged, cajoled, entreated, and thundered against the enemies of the Church, of peace, and of right action. In 1215 and
1216 Innocent was to take two major steps to achieve the goals
which he desired most. In 1215 he convened the Fourth Lateran Council, in which the work of earlier Church Councils
toward the definition of dogma and law was completed and
the reform of the Universal Church was, at least so it appeared, at last begun. At the end of the Council, Innocent
took up his second task. He proclaimed the Fifth Crusade,
which was to get underway in 1217, thereby, he hoped, bring-

---

1. Text in C. R. Cheney and W. H. Semple, eds., *Selected Letters of
Pope Innocent III concerning England (1198-1216)* (London, 1953), pp. 144-
145.

ing to completion his second great aim, the recovery of the Holy Land.

By 1198 the crusading Kingdom of Jerusalem had been reduced to a few towns on the Syrian coast whose lords and clergy continued to implore military aid from their fellow Christians in western Europe.[2] Jerusalem itself had fallen to the armies of Saladin in 1187, and the Third Crusade, which had proposed to regain it, ended in bickering and failure. Its leaders, the most powerful rulers in the West, had either died or returned to more pressing affairs at home. Frederick I Barbarossa, the Roman Emperor, had died before reaching the Holy Land. Richard I Lionheart, King of England, had been captured by the Duke of Austria while enroute home —in complete violation of his status as a Crusader—and held for an enormous ransom. King Philip II Augustus of France, having quarreled with Richard of England in the Holy Land, exploited Richard's captivity by encroaching upon the English king's possessions in France, thus continuing the drawn-out military conflict between the rulers of France and England which had begun half a century earlier and would continue for many more years. The failure of the Third Crusade did not, however, dampen Christendom's crusading ardor. The Holy Land and the Christians in it remained in dire peril, and each pope after 1187 declared that the Crusade stood at the center of his duties as the leader of Christendom. Not only popes, but itinerant preachers, poets, and crusade propagandists continued to lament the distress of the Christians in "The Lands Beyond the Sea." Secular as well as spiritual leaders proposed new crusading efforts. The Emperor Henry VI, the son of Frederick Barbarossa, was himself preparing to launch a massive offensive in the East when he died unexpectedly in 1197. In the following year, at a tournament at Ecry in France, a number of lay barons spontaneously took up the Cross.

2. For the general history of Christendom and Crusade during this period, see Kenneth M. Setton, ed., *A History of the Crusades;* Vol. I, *The First Hundred Years,* M. W. Baldwin, ed., and Vol. II, *The Later Crusades,* R. L. Wolfe and H. W. Hazard, eds. (reprint edition Madison, Wisc., 1969). See also Steven Runciman, *A History of the Crusades,* Vol. III, *The Kingdom of Acre and the Later Crusades* (paper, New York, 1967), pp. 3-236.

The conviction that the Christian lands in Syria and Palestine were of utmost importance to Europeans and that their loss was a sure sign of God's manifest displeasure with Christian society pervaded nearly all levels of thought in the period 1198–1229. Visionaries, lawyers, calculating and idealistic rulers, and calculating and idealistic popes expressed again and again the view that only by regaining the "Vision of Peace"—the allegorical meaning of Jerusalem—could Christian society be certain of divine favor. Yet this same Christian society faced other difficulties besides the loss of the Kingdom of Jerusalem to the Moslems. Since the eleventh century, religious dissent and unorthodox beliefs had appeared more frequently in western Europe itself, and the busy ecumenical and local Councils of the later twelfth century had begun the long process of the stricter definition of dogma which was to alienate yet more men from the Church. The problem of heresy, in fact, loomed no less large in 1198 than did the problem of the Holy Land. Nor did the dangers to orthodox belief and the integrity of the Church end with heresy. The late twelfth century had witnessed an enormous growth of both theoretical and actual power in the hands of the kings of Europe. The great struggle to free the Church and churchmen from lay domination, which had begun with the Investiture Contest in the late eleventh century, once again appeared to be headed toward defeat. Kings and lay lords encroached upon Church lands, and the Church often found itself with few defenses against these immediate threats. In the Kingdom of Sicily, for example, the vassals of the dead Emperor Henry VI so disregarded the Pope's rights of overlordship that one of Innocent III's first acts was, in utter desperation, to threaten the launching of a Crusade against them. In this case, the Crusade was a last, desperate measure. Between 1198 and 1229, however, it would become the only instrument upon which the popes could rely for widespread support—to recover the Holy Land, to combat heresy, or to defend the Church itself. In the process of turning the Crusade from the Holy Land, popes and secular rulers transformed the Crusade Idea itself.

The late twelfth century had in fact witnessed the last

stages of the crystallization of the Crusade Idea. The barons who had first heard the plea of Pope Urban II at the Council of Clermont in 1095 and had gone on what men then called the "pilgrimage" to the Holy Land had succeeded beyond their wildest expectations. Their hardships, defeats, unforeseen victories, and the final liberation of Jerusalem from the Moslems had given them the ineradicable impression of divine assistance and favor and had given Christendom a new institution, the Crusade. The divergent strands of intellectual and military experience which had done so much to shape the Crusade Idea before 1095 were woven together in the light of the experiences of the First Crusade, and slowly the unique and—men thought, miraculous—event was consciously duplicated. In 1144–1147 many of the themes of the historiography of the First Crusade were revived by the preachers of the Second Crusade. The spontaneous gestures of Pope Urban II—the declaration of the Truce of God, the offering of a Crusade indulgence, and formation of a rite for taking the Cross—became more precise and institutionalized. By the last years of the century there were categorical terms to designate both the men who fought in the Holy Land—*crucesignati*, Crusaders—and the enterprise upon which they ventured—*croseria*, Crusade. A formidable body of juristic theology explicitly defined crusader status in the eyes and the courts of the Church, and the vocabulary of crusading preachers had been ritualized by a century of slow formation and development of characteristic themes to invoke appropriate responses among the faithful.[3]

Not only did Christendom possess in the Crusade Idea an instrument uniquely suited to express its sense of oneness, but ecclesiastical development in the twelfth century had sharpened a sense among Europeans as a community of Christians and of the Church as the guardian and spiritual director of that community. At the head of Christendom stood the Pope. The twelfth century was not, strictly speaking, a century of "papal monarchy," but the increasingly authoritative tone of conciliar definitions of dogma, the role

3. On the evolution of the Crusade Idea, see E. O. Blake, "The Formation of the 'Crusade Idea,'" *Journal of Ecclesiastical History* 21 (1970), 11-31.

of popes in directing the activities of councils, and the place of the papacy in the increasingly articulate science of canon law continued to increase that papal prestige which the reform papacy of the mid eleventh century had begun. The only serious rival to papal authority had been the Roman emperor, and the twelfth century had witnessed, first in the person of Henry V (1105–1122) and later in that of Frederick Barbarossa (1154–1180) two strong challengers. Both representatives of the secular authority had given way before the spiritual authority of the papacy, however, and by 1198, although it did not claim the authority to *rule* in Christendom, the papacy had certainly emerged as the final arbiter of matters spiritual. Supported by a very efficient bureaucracy, its legal authority upheld by generations of skilled canon lawyers, and its claim as a spokesman of universal Christendom virtually unchallenged, the papacy assumed the voice of Christendom and reflected its most intense concerns.[4]

Although it had been a pope—Urban II—who had proclaimed the First Crusade in 1095, the direct control of crusade affairs had quickly slipped from papal hands into those of the barons who led their armies to the East. Although later crusades were also proclaimed by popes, their actual planning and execution was carried out by lay lords. The Second Crusade, for example, was led by the Emperor Conrad III and King Louis VII of France. The Third Crusade was led by Frederick Barbarossa, Richard Lionheart, and Philip Augustus. Even the proposed crusade of Henry VI was to be an imperial project, conceived, directed, and executed by a lay lord. Between 1198 and 1229, however, not only were popes to call out Crusades, but they were to make a more energetic effort to direct them. The fall of Jerusalem, the rise of a new Moslem power under Saladin, and Christians' contempt for squabbling kings who neglected God's business in order to further their own had diminished the glamor of crusade planners. The troubles between France and England after 1190, the problems surrounding the imperial elections of 1198 and

4. A good recent study is that of Geoffrey Barraclough, *The Medieval Papacy* (paper, New York, 1968). See also R. W. Southern, *Western Society and the Church in the Middle Ages* (Baltimore, paper, 1970).

1210, and the preoccupation of the north Italian cities with the expansion of their commercial empires had left no single ruler or group of rulers able or willing to assume direction of the Crusade. By default of the lay lords as much as by the prestige of its own position, the papacy emerged by 1198 as the only force which could organize and dispatch another expedition to the Holy Land.

Upon the death of Celestine III in 1198, Lothario de Conti was elected pope, taking the pontifical title Innocent III. Innocent had been an aristocrat, a papal administrator of a high order, and an accomplished lawyer. He was on good terms with the major powers of Christendom, and he knew better than anyone else how to exploit both papal authority and papal diplomacy. If Innocent, in his somber and tedious moral work *On the Contempt of the World,* had shown himself a mediocre moral philosopher, hardly the equal of the brilliant group of moral philosophers in Paris, his voluminous papal correspondence, his intricate legal decisions, and his firm sustaining of papal authority in times of crisis proved him a brilliant pope, one of the greatest the Church has ever had.[5] At no time since the pontificate of Urban II had the needs and resources of Christendom been in more able hands. At no time in history had the papacy at its disposal a more elaborate array of instruments of power nor a pope more perfectly prepared to use them. At no time had Christendom recognized its own needs so articulately: to establish peace among warring lords, to root out and destroy heresy, and to win back the Holy Land from the enemies of Christ.

None of these aims was completely achieved. Although Innocent denounced, interdicted, and excommunicated kings and emperors, wars among Christians went on, papal directives were flouted, and ecclesiastical resources were exploited flagrantly by lay rulers. Although Innocent launched three crusades during his short eighteen-year pontificate,

---

5. There is as yet no comprehensive work in English on Pope Innocent III. See L. E. Binns, *Innocent III* (London, 1931) and A. Luchaire, *Innocent III*, 6 vols. (Paris, 1905-1908). The only detailed study of Pope Innocent and the Crusade Idea is the recent work of Helmut Roscher, *Papst Innocenz III und die Kreuzzüge* (Göttingen, 1969).

none was successful, and the pope retained control of none. Although Innocent reconstituted the Inquisition, instituted new religious orders to combat heresy, and finally launched the Crusade in all its fury against heretics, heresy remained to plague the Church for centuries to come. The most able and intelligent of the popes had come to the throne of St. Peter at a time when ecclesiastical resources were strongest, at a time when rivalries among secular princes offered him many advantages, which he knew how to exploit. Yet neither Innocent III nor his successors were ever completely effective arbiters of secular affairs, and the Crusade, the most characteristic institution of univérsal Christendom, changed in their hands into an ineffective weapon which, by the middle of the thirteenth century, men had come to scorn. Indeed, the transformation of the Crusade Idea between 1198 and 1229 offers a complex and ironic commentary to papal success in other areas, and its history offers a useful viewpoint from which to regard the complex thirteenth-century world.

Innocent's earliest papal letters were full of talk of a forthcoming Crusade. In 1198 he began his preparations, and in 1202 the Fourth Crusade was launched. Immediately, however, things got out of control. The Crusaders, who had contracted with the Venetians for transport, could not provide enough men to fulfill their contract. The Venetians offered an alternative: the Crusaders could aid Venice in bringing a rebellious ally, the Christian city of Zara in Dalmatia, to heel. After the capture of Zara, yet another diversion appeared. An exiled candidate for the throne of the Empire at Constantinople asked Venetian aid in returning, and the crusaders attacked yet another Christian city, this time the holiest city in Christendom, thus bringing to an end the long-standing feud between western crusaders and Byzantines which had begun with the First Crusade. In 1204 the Crusaders and Venetians captured Constantinople and installed a Latin emperor. By 1207 they had ceased to call themselves "Crusaders," as they parceled out among themselves and their Venetian patrons the spoils of conquest.[6] Innocent, un-

6. The best survey of modern work on the Fourth Crusade is the excellent study by Donald Queller and Susan J. Stratton, "A Century of Controversy

daunted, began plans for yet another Crusade.

The increasing strength of heresy, particularly in the south of France, however, appeared even more pressing than the needs of the Holy Land. Not only did heretics openly flaunt their unorthodoxy, but in some areas, particularly the County of Toulouse, they appear to have been almost a majority. Innocent sent papal legates and missionaries to Toulouse, but the murder of the legate Peter of Castelnau in 1208 made the pope determine stronger measures. In the same year, for the first time, full Crusade privileges were offered to those who would take up arms against the heretics, and the first crusade against Christians, the Albigensian Crusade, was launched. It, too, slipped from papal control, however, and the bloodbath in southern France between 1209 and 1229 elicited expressions of horror not only from Christians elsewhere, but from churchmen themselves. If the crusade crushed heresy in southern France, it did not crush it elsewhere, and the chief profiteer from the enterprise was to be the king of France, who gained, by judicious exploitation of military force and legal authority, a large addition to his kingdom.[7] But the Crusade against Christians was not the only new direction which the Crusade Idea took during this period. In 1212 and 1213, large numbers of children in France

on the Fourth Crusade," *Studies in Medieval and Renaissance History*, Vol. 6 (Lincoln, Neb., 1969), 233-278. For Byzantine-Western relations at the end of the twelfth century see Charles M. Brand, *Byzantium Confronts the West, 1180-1204* (Cambridge Mass., 1968).

7. Much of the social temper of France around 1200 is vividly described in A. Luchaire, *Social France at the Time of Philip Augustus*, trans. E. Krehbiel (paper, New York, 1967). On the Albigensian Crusade, see the study of Austin Evans, "The Albigensian Crusade," in Vol. II of Setton, *A History of the Crusades*, pp. 277-324. More exhaustive studies are found in the works of Christine Thouzellier, *Catharisme et valdéisme en Languedoc* (2nd ed., Paris, 1969) and *Hérésie et hérétiques. Vaudois, cathares, patarins, albigeois* (Rome, 1969). A recent broader survey of the problems of medieval heresy is that edited by Jacques LeGoff, *Hérésies et sociétés dans l'Europe pré-industrielle. 11e-18e siècles*, Communications et débats du Colloque de Royaumont (Paris–La Haye, 1968). On the advantages to the crown of France, see Robert Fawtier, *The Capetian Kings of France* (paper, New York, 1965). See also A. P. Evans and W. L. Wakefield, *Heresies of the High Middle Ages*, Records of Civilization, Sources and Studies, Number LXXXI (New York, 1969).

and Germany left their homes, took to the roads, and made their way to the Mediterranean, some proposing to walk to the Holy Land across the sea, others certain that God would provide, not only transportation, but victory against the Moslems and the prize of Jerusalem itself. Although the Children's Crusade ended in disaster, the Pope himself remarked that the children shamed the leaders of Christendom and determined to launch yet another expedition.[8]

In 1215 the Fourth Lateran Council met in Rome. It culminated the work of the twelfth-century councils, firmly established a vast body of dogma and law, and asserted once again the supremacy of the pope within the Church. At the end of the Council, Pope Innocent once again proclaimed a Crusade and offered the widest-ranging Crusading privileges ever made. In 1217 several minor expeditions occurred in the Holy Land, but the main crusading effort resulting from the Council was the Fifth Crusade, directed this time against Damietta in Egypt. In 1218 the Crusade began, and it met with great initial success. Moslem rule was weakened, and the Crusaders' persistence was rewarded by the capture of the city of Damietta itself. Mistaken leadership, Moslem resistance, and the intransigence of Cardinal Pelagius the papal legate, however, soon turned the victory into a defeat, and the Crusaders withdrew from Damietta defeated and exhausted.

Much of the blame for the collapse of the Fifth Crusade was placed upon the failure of the Emperor Frederick II to come to Egypt with the ships and men he had promised. Indeed, Frederick had taken the Cross himself at his coronation at Aachen in 1215, but Pope Honorius III, Innocent's successor, granted Frederick delays from 1217 to 1222, and, after a two-year moratorium on crusades, still another delay until 1227. Frederick's preoccupations with imperial affairs in Germany and Sicily accounted for these requests. In 1225 Frederick married Isabelle de Brienne, heiress of the King-

8. On the Childrens' Crusade, see Dana C. Munro, "The Children's Crusade," *American Historical Review* 19 (1913-1914), 516-524, and Norman Zacour, "The Children's Crusade," in Volume II of Setton, *A History of the Crusades*, pp. 325-342.

dom of Jerusalem, and thus added a personal concern for the future of the Christian Holy Land to his imperial interest. On September 8, 1227, Frederick finally set out for Jerusalem, but illness forced him to turn back. This time, however, Honorius' successor, Pope Gregory IX, summarily excommunicated Frederick. It was as an excommunicate, then, that Frederick finally set out for the East in 1228. He proceeded first to Cyprus, where he alienated the Frankish barons by pressing his claims to the island, and then to Jerusalem, where, by careful diplomacy and intelligence, he arranged the restoration of Jerusalem to the Christians and a ten-year truce with the Moslem ruler of Egypt. Frederick's achievements were remarkable—and paradoxical. The efforts of the most powerful Christian rulers of Europe for half a century, those of emperors, popes, kings, and preachers, had failed to restore the Holy Land. Then, in 1229, an excommunicated emperor whom some men were already beginning to describe as the Antichrist and who had been forbidden to go on crusade while under the ban of excommunication, achieved bloodlessly what others had failed to achieve in rivers of blood. Little wonder that critics of the Crusades fastened upon Frederick's success and earlier papal failures to question the papal view of the Crusade.[9]

The period 1198–1229 witnessed many momentous changes in western Europe. In 1212 the battle of Las Navas de Tolosa marked the shift of power from Moslems to Christians in Spain. The French historian Yves Renouard has argued that two battles fought shortly thereafter had equally great roles in shaping the political and cultural divisions of Europe. The defeat of Aragon by Simon de Montfort and northern French knights at the battle of Muret in 1213 eliminated the prospect of an Aragonese-Toulousain Mediterranean empire, and the defeat of King John of England by Philip II of France at Bouvines in 1214 sealed the fate of the English Angevin Empire in France:

9. On the development of Crusade criticism, see Palmer Throop, *Criticism of the Crusade: A Study of Public Opinion and Crusade Propaganda* (Amsterdam, 1940). For the political aspects of Crusades in Europe, see Joseph R. Strayer, "The Political Crusades of the Thirteenth Century," in Volume II of Setton, *A History of the Crusades*, pp. 343-375.

After the years 1212, 1213, 1214, it is clear that western Europe was destined to be exclusively Christian and that it was to be divided into three groupings largely defined by the great geographical divisions: the Kingdom of England to the north of the Channel, the Kingdom of France between the Channel and the Pyrenees, and the Spanish kingdoms to the south of the Pyrenees.[10]

By these years, the fragmented imperial authority in Germany and north Italy already revealed those political divisions which were to characterize these lands until the nineteenth century, and the imperial power in the Hohenstaufen kingdom of Sicily was to be broken forever within a half century. The urbanization of Europe achieved great impetus during this period, and both the religious sensibilities of laymen and the institution of universities reflect city-culture and its new role in Christendom. The canons of the Fourth Lateran Council in 1215 summarily defined dogma and ecclesiastical law. The experience of the Crusade Idea in this period thus contributes another view of a process which was to have great consequences in the succeeding two centuries. The experience of actual Crusades reflects both an awareness of universal Christendom and the slow beginnings of the secular culture and political organization of Europe.

The sources chosen to illustrate the transformation of the Crusade Idea during the period 1198–1229 themselves reflect the changing character of Christendom. The chief sources for the history of the Fourth Crusade are two chronicles written in Old French, one by one of the leaders of the Crusade, Geoffrey de Villehardouin, the other by a simple knight, Robert de Clari. Each reflects the layman's view of the Crusade Idea, of Constantinople, and the experiences of the Fourth Crusade in a different way, and together they constitute the most valuable body of documentation of lay opinion on a single crucial event in the Middle Ages. Various

10. Yves Renouard, "1212-1216. Comment les traits durables de l'Europe occidentale moderne se sont définis au début du XIIIe siècle," in his *Etudes d'histoire médiévale* (Paris, 1968), Vol. I, 77-91 at 91.

letters by Pope Innocent III illustrate both papal means of communication and the attitude of the Pope to the surprising capture of Constantinople. Brief extracts from Latin chronicles illustrate the relic-hunting which made Constantinople such a profitable conquest in both the material and spiritual sense.

The Albigensian Crusade is described by the great English chronicler Roger of Wendover, who was a contemporary of the events described and was well informed about them. His account offers a view of the Crusade against Christians as it appeared to a neutral churchman not directly involved in the action. The sources cited to illustrate the Children's Crusade are drawn from two chroniclers, the bemused Continuator of the Cologne Chronicle and the savagely hostile Matthew Paris, the successor to Roger of Wendover as chronicler at the monastery of St. Albans. Selections from Pope Innocent III's announcement of the crusading privilege at the Fourth Lateran Council mark the papal resumption of the Crusade Idea after the fall of Constantinople and the debacle of the Albigensian Crusade. The description of the council by Roger of Wendover again illustrates the appearance of a major event to a chronicler contemporary with it.

The Fifth Crusade is described by the inclusion of an entire literary work, the chronicle of Oliver of Paderborn, the *Historia Damiatina*, which its translator, Rev. Joseph J. Gavigan, has entitled *The Capture of Damietta*. Oliver was a teacher in the cathedral school at Cologne, a preacher of the crusade in 1214–1216, and an eyewitness at the Fourth Lateran Council in 1215. In 1216 Oliver sailed on the Fifth Crusade himself, and he wrote *The Capture of Damietta* between 1217 and 1222, that is, while actually on the Crusade. Oliver returned to Cologne after the fall of Damietta and resumed the preaching of the Crusade. He became Bishop of Paderborn in 1225 and Cardinal of Santa Sabina shortly thereafter. His last years were spent preparing for the Crusade of 1227, the year in which he died. Oliver's chronicle is complemented by three letters written from the East during the

Crusade, all of them taken from the chronicle of Roger of Wendover.

Roger of Wendover also describes the movement for a new Crusade in 1227 and offers a favorable account of Frederick II's Crusade in 1228–1229. Philip of Novara, an Italian in the service of the Ibelin family, one of the most powerful families among the Syrian Franks, was a bitter opponent of the emperor, and the selection from his chronicle dealing with Frederick's Crusade is uniformly hostile. Two further views complete the complex picture of the crusading Emperor. Frederick's own letter to King Henry III of England gives his usual dramatic and imposing view of his own success, but the letter from Gerold, Patriarch of Jerusalem, offers a view much closer to that of Philip of Novara. The contrasting tones of Frederick's and Gerold's letters in 1229 sums up effectively the ambiguity of the Crusade Idea during this period. The Crusade had been turned against Christian Byzantines and heretics, children had taken the cross and been destroyed, and an excommunicated emperor had won lands which a century of kings and saints had failed to win.

The transformation of crusade ideas and institutions was reflected in Christian consciousness on yet another level. Literary opposition to the Crusade begins to strengthen in the early thirteenth century. The Provençal poet Guillem Figueira savagely denounced both the Fourth and the Albigensian Crusades:

> Deceitful Rome, avarice ensnares you, so that you shear the wool of your sheep too much. May the Holy Ghost, who takes on human flesh, hear my prayer and break your beak, O Rome! You will never have a truce with me because you are false and perfidious with us and with the Greeks.

> Rome, you do little harm to the Saracens, but you massacre Greeks and Latins. In hell-fire and ruin you have your seat, Rome.

Figueira lashed out at the disaster of the Fifth Crusade as well:

Rome, you know well that your base cheating and folly caused the loss of Damietta. Evil leader, Rome! God will strike you down because you govern too falsely through money, O Rome of evil race and evil compact.[11]

The papal condemnation of Frederick II's Crusade met with equal vilification. The growth of criticism of the Crusade parallelled the changes in the conception and uses to which the Crusade was put between 1198 and 1229. Although the Crusade Idea was to remain strong throughout the thirteenth and early fourteenth centuries, opposition to the Crusade was to grow stronger. The crusade attempts of King Louis IX of France later in the century and the enthusiastic crusade schemes of Pope Gregory X and the Second Council of Lyons in 1274 were echoed later by the elaborate Crusade plans produced in the fourteenth century, for example those of Marino Sanudo and Pierre du Bois. Yet even orthodox churchmen, men such as Ramon Lull and Roger Bacon, were to question the legitimacy of the entire concept of Crusade. All later Crusade projects—as well as all later Crusade criticism—were to reflect the character of the years 1198–1229 as a time of change, both in Christian society and in the Crusade Idea.[12]

The Editor wishes to thank the Marquette University Press for permission to quote from James A. Brundage, *The Crusades; A Documentary Survey*, the letter of Innocent III on p. 41 and the selection on the Children's Crusade on p. 35; and the Columbia University Press for permission to quote from John L. La Monte, trans., *The Wars of Frederick II against the Ibelins in Syria and Cyprus* by Philip de Novare, for the excerpts from Philip of Novara's *History* on pp. 156-161.

11. Throop, *op. cit.*, pp. 31-50.
12. The most complete bibliography of the Crusades in English is that of Aziz S. Atiya, *The Crusade: Historiography and Bibliography* (Bloomington, Ind., 1962). More recent scholarship has been surveyed by James A. Brundage, "Recent Developments in Crusade Historiography," *Catholic Historical Review* 49 (1964), 493-507. The authors of individual sources printed below are identified in the introductions to individual sections.

I. The Fourth Crusade, 1202-1207

1. Selections from the Chronicles of Villehardouin, Robert de Clari, Gunther, and Nicetas

The following selections from the several chronicles which describe the Fourth Crusade illustrate the wide range of views which even contemporaries had of the remarkable events which occurred between 1202 and 1207. Villehardouin and Robert de Clari offer the views of westerners of high and low rank, Gunther illustrates the craze for relics which possessed the crusaders once inside Constantinople, and the brief selection from Nicetas illustrates the Byzantine impression of the fall of the city.

Geoffrey of Villehardouin was born around 1155. He was connected by birth and marriage with many of the nobility of Champagne, participated in the tournament of Ecry in 1199, and went to Venice to negotiate with the Venetians for the transportation of the members of the Fourth Crusade. Having participated in the sieges of Zara and Constantinople, Villehardouin remained in the newly founded Latin Empire and was given estates in the Peloponnesus. He died around 1213. His point of view in his narrative is uniformly an aristocratic one, and his is the best account of at least the "official" attitude of the Crusaders during their remarkable adventures on the Adriatic and the Bosphorus. The best modern edition of Villehardouin is that of Edmond Faral, Villehardouin: La Conquête de Constantinople, 2 vols. (*Paris,* 1938). *There is a complete English translation by Sir Frank Marzials,* Memoirs of the Crusades by Villehardouin and De Joinville (*New York, 1958). See also Jeannette M. A. Beer,* Villehardouin: Epic Historian (*Geneva, 1968*).

Robert de Clari, on the other hand, was a simple soldier, the son of a vassal of Pierre of Amiens, who dictated his story to a monk, probably around 1216. Robert was not in the decision-making process, as was Villehardouin, but a knight, one of those who formed the bulk of the crusading forces. Robert's account is thus an eyewitness version of the events, at once more lively and less well informed than Villehardouin's. There is an excellent English translation of Robert's chronicle by Edgar H. McNeal, The Conquest of Constantinople *(paper, New York, 1969).*

Nicetas Choniates and Gunther of Paris, two contemporary chroniclers, offer brief selections dealing with the Byzantine sense of outrage and the Crusaders' mania for relics, both reflecting powerful emotional overtones to the conquest.

The texts in this section, with the exception of the first selection from Villehardouin and the last selection from the Letters of Pope Innocent III, are contained in Dana C. Munro, ed. and trans., The Fourth Crusade *(University of Pennsylvania Translations and Reprints from the Original Sources of European History, Vol. III, No. 1) Philadelphia, 1901. The selection here is complete, except for Munro's editorial apparatus and bibliography. The first selection from Villehardouin has been translated by the Editor.*

The Calling of the Fourth Crusade: The Barons (Villehardouin)

Know ye that eleven hundred and ninety-seven years after the Incarnation of Our Lord Jesus Christ, when Innocent (III) was Pope at Rome and Philip (II) King of France and Richard (I) King of England, there was in France a holy man who was called Fulk of Neuilly (this Neuilly is between Langny-sur-Marne and Paris) who was a priest and held a parish in that town. And this Fulk of whom I speak began to preach across the Ile-de-France and the surrounding areas, and Our Lord performed many miracles through him.

Know also that the fame of this holy man spread as far as the court of the Pope at Rome, and the Pope sent to France and ordered this good man to preach the Cross by papal authority. Shortly after, the Pope sent one of his cardinals, Master Pierre de Chappes, a crusader, to offer an indulgence which I will describe to you: all those who crossed themselves and took up the service of God during one year of a military expedition would be acquitted of all the sins they had committed and of which they had confessed themselves. Because this indulgence was so great, the hearts of men were much moved, and many took up the Cross because of the great indulgence.

The year after Fulk began to preach, there was held a tournament in Champagne, at a chateau called Ecry. And by the grace of God it happened that Thibaut, Count of Champagne and Brie, took the Cross himself as did Count Louis of Blois and Chartrain. And this was at the beginning of Advent. Now know also that this Count Thibaut was a young man, no older than twenty-two years of age, and Louis was no older than twenty-seven . . .

With these two counts there joined as crusaders many high barons of France: including Simon de Montfort and Renaud de Montmirail. Great was the excitement across all lands when these great men took up the Cross.

The Compact with the Venetians (Villehardouin)

"Sire, we have come to you in behalf of the noble barons of France who have taken the cross in order to avenge the shame of Jesus Christ and to reconquer Jerusalem, if God will permit. And because they know no people who are as able to assist them as you and your people, they pray you, for God's sake, to pity the land of *Outre-mer* and the shame of Jesus Christ, and to endeavor to furnish them transports and ships of war."

"Under what conditions?" asked the doge.

"Under any conditions that you may propose or advise, if they are able to fulfill them," replied the messengers.

"Certainly," replied the doge, [to his associates] "it is a great undertaking that they have asked of us and they seem to be considering an important matter"; [to the messengers] "we will give you an answer in a week, and do not wonder if the time seems long, for such a great undertaking deserves much thought."

At the time fixed by the doge, they returned to the palace. I can not tell you all that was said, but the conclusion of the conference was as follows:

"My lords," said the doge, "we will tell you what we have decided, if we can get the Grand Council and the people of the country to agree to it; and you shall decide whether you can fulfill your part.

"We will furnish *huissiers*[1] for carrying 4,500 horses and 9,000 esquires, and vessels for 4,500 knights and 20,000 foot-soldiers. The agreement shall be to furnish food for nine months for all these horses and men. That is the least that we will do, on condition that we are paid four marks per horse and two marks per man.

"And we will observe all these conditions which we explain to you, for one year, beginning the day we leave the harbor of Venice to fight in the service of God and of Christianity, wherever we may go. The sum of these payments indicated above amounts to 85,000 marks.

"And we will do still more: we will add fifty armed galleys, for the love of God; on the condition that as long as our alliance shall last, of every conquest of land or money that we make, by sea or land, we shall have one-half and you the other. Now deliberate whether you can fulfill these conditions."

The messengers went away, saying that they would talk it over and reply the next day. They consulted and discussed that night and then resolved to agree to it. The next day they went to the doge and said: "Sire, we are ready to make this agreement." The doge said that he would speak to his people and tell them the result.

It was explained in council that they would go to Babylon,[2] because at Babylon they could do more injury to the Turks

---

1. *Huissiers* were vessels having a door, *huis*, in the stern, which could be opened so as to take in the horses.
2. Cairo.

than anywhere else. And in public it was announced that they would go across the sea. It was then Lent [March, 1201], and on St. John's day the following year, the 1202nd year after the Incarnation of Jesus Christ, the barons and pilgrims were to be at Venice and the vessels were to be ready on their arrival.

Compact of the Venetians with the Sultan of Babylon
(l'Estoire d'Eracles Empereur)

[A.D. 1199?] After this he [the sultan of Babylon] summoned messengers and servants and sent them to Venice, loaded with great wealth and great riches. He sent them to the doge and gave beautiful presents to the Venetians, and commanded the latter, if they could do so, not to go to the land of Egypt; he would give them great treasures and many privileges in the port of Alexandria. The messengers went to Venice, did as they were commanded, and returned as quickly as possible.

The Crusaders Unable to Pay the Venetians
(Robert de Clari)

. . . While the pilgrims were staying on the island of St. Nicholas,[1] the doge of Venice and the Venetians went to speak to them and demanded the pay for the Navy which had been prepared. And the doge said to them that they had acted wrongly in commanding through their messengers that vessels should be prepared for 4,000 knights and their equipment, and for 100,000 foot-soldiers. Of these 4,000 knights, there were not more than 1,000 present, for the others had gone to other ports. And of these 100,000 foot-soldiers there were not more than 50,000 or 60,000. "Nevertheless," said the doge, "we want you to pay us the sum which you promised." When the crusaders heard this, they debated and arranged that each knight should pay four marks and four marks for each horse, and each esquire two

1. The Lido.

marks; and those who paid less, should pay one mark. When they collected this money, they paid it to the Venetians. But 50,000 marks still remained due.

When the doge and the Venetians saw that the pilgrims had not paid more, they were all so incensed that the doge said to the pilgrims: "My lords, you have imposed upon us shamefully. For, as soon as your messengers had made the agreement with me and my people, I issued orders throughout my whole land that no merchant should undertake a voyage, but all were to aid in preparing this fleet. They have been waiting ever since and have gained nothing for the last year and a half; and, accordingly, they have lost much. Therefore my men and I want you to pay us the money which you owe us. If you do not pay us, you shall not leave this island before we get our money; and no one shall bring you anything to eat or drink." The doge, however, was a very excellent man and did not prevent the people from bringing enough food and drink.

When the count and the crusaders heard what the doge said they were much troubled and grieved. They made another collection and borrowed all the money they could from those who were thought to have any. They paid it all to the Venetians, but after this payment 36,000 marks still remained due. They said to the Venetians that they had been imposed upon; that the army was greatly impoverished by this last collection; that they could not pay any more money at all, for they had hardly enough to support the army.

When the doge perceived that they could not pay all the money and that they were in sore straits, he said to his people: "Sirs, if we let these people go back to their own country, we shall always be considered base and tricky. Let us go to them and say that, if they are willing to pay us the 36,000 marks which they owe us out of their part of the first conquests which we make, we will carry them across the sea." The Venetians were well pleased with the doge's proposition. Accordingly, they went to the camp of the pilgrims. When they came thither, the doge said to the crusaders: "Sires, we have agreed, I and my people, that if you are willing to guarantee faithfully to pay us the 36,000 marks, which you owe us, out of your share of the first conquests, we will carry you across the sea."

When the crusaders heard what the doge proposed they were very glad and fell at his feet for joy. They bound themselves very willingly to do faithfully what the doge had proposed. They were so joyous that night that there was no one so poor that he did not make a great illumination, and each one carried great torches made of candles on the end of his lance, both outside of the camp and inside, so that the whole army seemed intoxicated.

The New Agreement with the Venetians (Robert de Clari)

Afterwards the doge came to the army and said: "Sirs, it is now winter, we cannot cross the sea, nor does this depend upon me. For I would have had you cross already, if it had not depended upon you. But let us do the best we can. There is a city near here, named Zara. The people of this city have done us much evil, and I and my men want to punish them, if we can. If you will take my advice, we will go there this winter and stay until Easter. Then we will make ready our navy and go to *Outre-mer* at Lady-day. The city of Zara is very rich and well supplied with all kinds of provisions." The barons and the nobles among the crusaders agreed to what the doge proposed. But no one in the army knew this plan, except the leaders.

The Capture of Zara (Villehardouin)

The day after the feast of St. Martin,[1] some people from Zara came to speak to the doge of Venice, who was in his tent. They said to him that they would surrender the city and all their property to his mercy, if their lives were spared. The doge said that he would not accept these or any other conditions without the advice of the counts and barons, and that he would go and discuss the matter with them.

While he went to talk to the counts and barons, that party,

1. Nov. 12, 1202.

of which I have already spoken, who wanted to break up the army, said to the messengers: "Why do you want to surrender your city? The pilgrims will not attack you and you have nothing to fear from them. If you can defend yourselves against the Venetians, you need have no anxiety." And they sent one of them, Robert de Boves, who went to the walls of the city and announced the same thing. So the messengers returned to the city and the plan of surrender was given up.

The doge of Venice, when he came to the counts and barons, said to them: "Sirs, the people yonder want to surrender the city to my mercy, on condition that their lives be spared. But I will not make this agreement or any other without your advice." The barons replied: "Sire, we advise you to make this agreement and we pray you to do so." He said he would, and they all went back together to the doge's tent to make this agreement. They found that the messengers had gone away, following the advice of those who wanted to break up the army.

Then the abbot of Vaux of the order of Citeaux rose and said to them: "Sirs, I forbid you, in the name of the Pope at Rome, to attack this city; for the inhabitants are Christians and you are pilgrims." When the doge heard this he was much irritated and troubled. He said to the counts and barons: "Sirs, this city was practically in my power, and your people have taken it from me; you had promised that you would aid me in conquering it; now I require you to do so."

Then the counts and barons and those who belonged to their party held a conference and said: "Those who have prevented this agreement have committed a very great outrage, and it was not right for them to try to break up the army. Now we shall be disgraced, if we do not aid in capturing the city." They went to the doge and said to him: "Sire, we will aid you in capturing the city, in spite of those who wish to prevent it."

Accordingly the city was surrendered to the mercy of the doge of Venice, on condition that the lives of the inhabitants should be spared. Then the doge went to the counts and barons and said to them: "Sirs, we have conquered this city, by the grace of God and through your aid. It is now winter and we can not leave here until Easter. For we should find no provisions elsewhere; and this city is very rich and very well supplied with everything needful. Let us divide it accordingly into two parts; we will take one-half of it and you the other half."

The Summons to Alexis (Robert de Clari)

In the meantime the crusaders and the Venetians remained at Zara during the winter. They considered how great the expense had been and said to one another that they could not go to Babylon or Alexandria or Syria; for they had neither provisions nor money for the journey. They had already used up everything they had, either during the sojourn that they had made or in the great price that they had paid for the vessels. They said that they could not go and, even if they should go, they would accomplish nothing; they had neither provisions nor money sufficient to support them.

The doge of Venice saw clearly that the pilgrims were ill at ease. He addressed them, saying: "Sirs, Greece is a very rich land and bountifully supplied with everything. If we can find a sufficient excuse for going there and taking food and other things, so as to recuperate ourselves, it would seem to me advisable, and then we could easily go across the sea." Then the marquis[1] rose and said: "Sir, I was in Germany at the emperor's[2] court last Christmas. There I saw a young man who was the emperor's brother in law.[3] This young man was the son of the emperor Kyrsac[4] of Constantinople from whom his brother had taken the empire of Constantinople by treason. Whoever could get this young man," said the marquis, "could certainly go to the land of Constantinople and take provisions and other things; for this young man is the rightful heir."

1. Boniface, marquis of Montferrat, the leader of the crusaders.
2. Philip of Suabia.
3. Alexis IV., brother of the queen Irene.
4. Isaac (II.) Angelos.

The Proposition made by King Philip (Villehardouin)

. . . "My lords, king Philip sends us to you and sends also
the son of the emperor of Constantinople, who is his wife's
brother.

"My lords, says the king, I shall send you my wife's brother;
I place him in the hands of God (may He preserve him from
death!), and in your hands. Since you are fighting for God, for
the right and for justice, you ought, if it lies in your power,
to restore to their inheritance those who have been wrong-
fully dispossessed. He [Alexis] will make with you the best
agreement which has ever been made by any one, and he
will give you the most powerful aid in conquering the land
of *Outre-mer.*

"In the first place, if God permits you to restore him to his
inheritance, he will put all the empire of Romania under the
obedience of Rome, from which it has been separated for a
long time. In the second place, he knows that you have spent
your property and that you are poor; he will give you 200,000
marks of silver and provisions for all the members of the
army, humble and noble. He will himself go with you to the
land of Babylon or will send thither with you (if you think it
better) 10,000 men at his expense. This service he will perform for you during one year. And so long as he lives, he will
maintain at his own expense 500 knights in the land of *Outre-
mer,* to guard the land.

"My lords, we have full power," said the messengers, "to
make this agreement, if you wish to do so. And be sure that
such a fine offer was never made to any one, and he who
refuses this can have no great desire to conquer." The leaders
said that they would discuss the matter, and an assembly was
appointed for the next day. When the host had assembled
this offer was presented to them.

There it was hotly discussed, "pro and con." The abbot of
Vaux of the order of Citeaux and the party that wanted to
break up the army said that they would not agree to it; it was
fighting against Christians; they had not set out for this purpose, but they wanted to go to Syria.

The other party replied: "Good sirs, in Syria you can do

nothing, you can see that clearly from those who have left us and gone to other ports. You know that it is through the land of Babylon or through Greece that the land of *Outre-mer* will be reconquered, if it is ever recovered. If we refuse this offer, we shall always be ashamed."

The army was in discord just as you have heard. And do not wonder that the laymen could not agree; for the white monks of the order of Citeaux in the army were also in discord. The abbot of Loos, who was a very holy and excellent man, and the other abbots who agreed with him, preached to the people and cried out to them to have mercy, saying that, for God's sake, they ought to keep the army together and to make this agreement; "for it is the best means of recovering the land of *Outre-mer.*" And the abbot of Vaux in his turn, and those who agreed with him, preached very frequently and said that that was all wrong; that they ought to go to the land of Syria and do what they could.

Then the marquis Boniface of Montferrat, Baldwin, count of Flanders and Hainault, count Louis and count Hugh of St. Pol and those who belonged to their party went and said that they would make this agreement; for they would be ashamed to refuse it. So they went to the doge's lodging and the messengers were summoned. They concluded the agreement, just as you have heard it above, by their oaths and by sealed compacts.

And in regard to this matter, the book tells you that there were only twelve of the French who made their oaths; and they could not get any more. Of these, the first was the marquis of Montferrat, count Baldwin of Flanders, count Louis of Blois and Chartres, the count of St. Pol, and eight others who agreed with them. So the compact was made, the securities given, and the time fixed when the heir of Constantinople should come; it was to be a fortnight after Easter.

The Discussion after the Arrival of Alexis (*Robert de Clari*)

Then all the barons of the army and the Venetians were summoned. When they had all assembled, the doge of Venice rose and said to them: "My lords, we have now a sufficient excuse for going to Constantinople, if you think it wise, for we have the lawful heir." Now some who did not want to go to Constantinople, spoke thus: "Bah! what are we going to do at Constantinople? We have our pilgrimage to make and intend to go to Babylon or Alexandria. Our ships are rented for only one year and the year is already half over."

The others said in reply: "What are we going to do at Babylon or Alexandria, since we have neither provisions nor money enough to go? It is better to go where we have a sufficient excuse for obtaining money and provisions by conquest, than to go where we shall die of hunger. Then we can do it, and he offers to go with us and to pay for our ships and our navy another year at his own expense." And the marquis of Montferrat did all in his power to urge our going to Constantinople, because he wished to take vengeance for a wrong which the emperor of Constantinople had done him.

The First Payment (Robert de Clari)

Afterwards all the barons assembled one day at the palace of the emperor[1] and demanded of him their pay. He replied that he would pay them, but he wished first to be crowned. Accordingly they made preparations and set a day for the coronation. On that day he was crowned emperor with due ceremony, with the consent of his father, who willingly granted it. After he had been crowned the barons demanded their pay. He said he would very willingly pay what he could and at that time he paid 100,000 marks. Of this sum the Venetians received one-half; for they were to receive one-half of the conquests. Of the 50,000 which remained, 36,000, which the Franks still owed for the vessels, were paid to the Venetians. And all those who had advanced money to pay for the passage were paid out of the 14,000 marks which the pilgrims had left.

1. Alexis. The crusaders rarely speak of Isaac as emperor.

The Public Defiance (Villehardouin)

They dismounted from their horses at the gate, entered the palace and found the emperor Alexis and the emperor Isaac, his father, seated upon two thrones, side by side. Near them was seated the empress, who was the father's wife, the son's step-mother, and the sister of the king of Hungary; a beautiful and good lady. A great number of nobles were with them; and it certainly seemed the court of a rich prince.

According to the agreement with the other messengers,[1] Conon of Bethune, who was very rich and very eloquent, spoke: "Sire, we have been sent to you by the barons of the army and by the doge of Venice. Know that they reproach you because of the great service which they have done you, which everybody knows and which is apparent to you. You have sworn to them, you and your father, to keep the agreement that you have made with them; and they have your written compact. You have not kept your agreement with them as you ought.

"They have summoned you many times, and we summon you in their name, before all your barons, to keep the agreement which you have made with them. If you do so, all will be well; if you do not keep it, know that in the future they will consider you neither as lord nor as friend; but they will try to get their rights in any way they can. They announce to you that they would injure neither you, nor any one else, before the defiance; for they have never acted treasonably, and in their country it is not the custom to do so. You have heard what we have said to you and you can do as you please."

The Greeks marveled much at this defiance and great insult. They said that no one had ever been so bold before as to defy the emperor of Constantinople in his own halls. The emperor Alexis looked savagely at the messengers, and so did all the Greeks, though they had on many occasions in the past looked very friendly.

1. Villehardouin was one of the messengers.

The Doge's Threat (Robert de Clari)

At these words the barons left the palace and returned to their camp. After returning they deliberated upon the course to follow. Meanwhile they sent two knights to the emperor and demanded again that he should pay them. He replied to the messengers that he would pay nothing, he had already paid too much, and that he was not afraid of any one. He also commanded them to go away and leave his land; they were to understand that if they did not depart, he would injure them. Then the messengers went back and told the barons the emperor's reply. When the barons heard this, they deliberated as to what they should do. The doge said that he wanted to speak to the emperor.

He sent a messenger to demand that the emperor should come to the harbor to speak to him. The emperor went on horseback. The doge prepared four armed galleys; he went in one and took the other three for protection. When he was near the shore he saw the emperor who had come on horseback. He addressed the latter as follows: "Alexis, what do you think you are going to do? Remember we have raised you from a very humble estate. We have made you lord and crowned you emperor. Will you not keep your agreement with us and will you not do more?" "No," replied the emperor, "I will not do anything more." "No?" said the doge, "wretched boy, we have raised you from the mire,[1] and we will throw you into the mire again; and be sure that I will do you all the injury that I can, from this time on."

The Sermons before the Final Attack on Constantinople (Robert de Clari)

When the pilgrims saw this,[2] they were very angry and grieved much; they went back from the other side of the harbor to their lodgings. When the barons had returned and had gotten ashore, they assembled and were much amazed, and said that it was on account of their sins that they did not

1. A coarse expression in the original.
2. That the attack was repulsed.

succeed in anything and could not capture the city. Meanwhile the bishops and the clergy in the army debated and decided that the war was a righteous one, and that they certainly ought to attack the Greeks. For formerly the inhabitants of the city had been obedient to the law of Rome and now they were disobedient, since they said that the law of Rome was of no account, and called all who believed in it "dogs." And the bishops said that for this reason one ought certainly to attack them, and that it was not a sin, but an act of great charity.

Then it was announced to all the host that all the Venetians and every one else should go and hear the sermons on Sunday morning;[1] and they did so. Then the bishops preached to the army, the bishop of Soissons, the bishop of Troyes, the bishop of Havestaist[2] master Jean Faicette,[3] and the abbot of Loos, and they showed to the pilgrims that the war was a righteous one; for the Greeks were traitors and murderers, and also disloyal, since they had murdered their rightful lord, and were worse than Jews. Moreover, the bishops said that, by the authority of God and in the name of the pope, they would absolve all who attacked the Greeks. Then the bishops commanded the pilgrims to confess their sins and receive the communion devoutly; and said that they ought not to hesitate to attack the Greeks, for the latter were enemies of God. They also commanded that all the evil women should be sought out and sent away from the army to a distant place. This was done; the evil women were all put on a vessel and were sent very far away from the army.

The Compact of Division (Villehardouin)

Then the members of the host debated and consulted upon the best course to pursue. The discussion was long and stormy, but the following was the result of the deliberation: If God granted that they should capture the city, all the booty that was taken should be brought together and divided fairly,

1. Apr. 11, 1204.
2. Halberstadt.
3. De Noyon, chancellor of Baldwin of Flanders.

as was fitting. And, if they captured the city, six[1] men should be chosen from the Franks[2] and six from the Venetians; these were to take oath upon relics that they would elect as emperor him whom they should judge to be the most useful for the good of the land. And he whom they chose as emperor should have one-quarter of all the conquests both in the city and outside; and in addition he should have the palace of the Lion's mouth and of Blachern. The other three-quarters should be divided into two parts, one-half for the Venetians and one-half for the crusaders. Then twelve from the wisest of the army of the pilgrims and twelve of the Venetians should be chosen to divide the fiefs and the offices among the men and to define the feudal service which each one owed to the emperor.

This compact was guaranteed and sworn to both by the Franks and the Venetians, with the condition that any one who wished could go away within one year from the end of March. Those who remained in the country must perform the feudal service to the emperor, as it might be arranged. Then the compact was made and sworn to and all who should not keep it were excommunicated by the clergy.

Account of the Sack (Nicetas)

. . . How shall I begin to tell of the deeds wrought by these nefarious men! Alas, the images, which ought to have been adored, were trodden under foot! Alas, the relics of the holy martyrs were thrown into unclean places! Then was seen what one shudders to hear, namely, the divine body and blood of Christ was spilled upon the ground or thrown about. They snatched the precious reliquaries, thrust into their bosoms the ornaments which these contained, and used the broken remnants for pans and drinking cups—precursors of Anti-christ, authors and heralds of his nefarious deeds which we momentarily expect. Manifestly, indeed, by that race then, just as formerly, Christ was robbed and insulted and His garments were divided by lot; only one thing was lacking,

1. Robert de Clari says ten.
2. A collective name for all the crusaders.

that His side, pierced by a spear, should pour rivers of divine blood on the ground.

Nor can the violation of the Great Church[1] be listened to with equanimity. For the sacred altar, formed of all kinds of precious materials and admired by the whole world, was broken into bits and distributed among the soldiers, as was all the other sacred wealth of so great and infinite splendor.

When the sacred vases and utensils of unsurpassable art and grace and rare material, and the fine silver, wrought with gold, which encircled the screen of the tribunal and the ambo, of admirable workmanship, and the door and many other ornaments, were to be borne away as booty, mules and saddled horses were led to the very sanctuary of the temple. Some of these which were unable to keep their footing on the splendid and slippery pavement, were stabbed when they fell, so that the sacred pavement was polluted with blood and filth.

Nay more, a certain harlot, a sharer in their guilt, a minister of the furies, a servant of the demons, a worker of incantations and poisonings, insulting Christ, sat in the patriarch's seat, singing an obscene song and dancing frequently. Nor, indeed, were these crimes committed and others left undone, on the ground that these were of lesser guilt, the others of greater. But with one consent all the most heinous sins and crimes were committed by all with equal zeal. Could those, who showed so great madness against God Himself, have spared the honorable matrons and maidens or the virgins consecrated to God?

Nothing was more difficult and laborious than to soften by prayers, to render benevolent, these wrathful barbarians, vomiting forth bile at every unpleasing word, so that nothing failed to inflame their fury. Whoever attempted it was derided as insane and a man of intemperate language. Often they drew their daggers against any one who opposed them at all or hindered their demands.

No one was without a share in the grief. In the alleys, in the streets, in the temples, complaints, weeping, lamentations,

1. St. Sophia.

grief, the groaning of men, the shrieks of women, wounds, rape, captivity, the separation of those most closely united. Nobles wandered about ignominiously, those of venerable age in tears, the rich in poverty. Thus it was in the streets, on the corners, in the temple, in the dens, for no place remained unassailed or defended the suppliants. All places everywhere were filled full of all kinds of crime. Oh, immortal God, how great the afflictions of the men, how great the distress!

Abbot Martin's Theft of Relics (Gunther)

While the victors were rapidly plundering the conquered city, which was theirs by right of conquest, the abbot Martin began to cogitate about his own share of the booty, and lest he alone should remain empty-handed, while all the others became rich, he resolved to seize upon plunder with his own sacred hands. But, since he thought it not meet to handle any booty of worldly things with those sacred hands, he began to plan how he might secure some portion of the relics of the saints, of which he knew there was a great quantity in the city.

Accordingly, having a presentiment of some great result, he took with him one of his two chaplains and went to a church[1] which was held in great reverence because in it the mother[2] of the most famous emperor Manuel[3] had a noble grave, which seemed of importance to the Greeks, but ours held for naught. There a very great amount of money brought in from all the surrounding country was stored, and also precious relics which the vain hope of security had caused them to bring in from the neighboring churches and monasteries. Those whom the Greeks had driven out, had told us of this before the capture of the city. When many pilgrims broke into this church and some were eagerly engaged in stealing gold and silver, others precious stones, Martin, thinking it unbecoming to commit sacrilege except in a

1. The church of Pantokrator.
2. Irene, died 1124.
3. Manuel (I.) Komnenos.

holy cause, sought a more retired spot where the very sanctity of the place seemed to promise that what he desired might be found.

There he found an aged man of agreeable countenance, having a long and hoary beard, a priest, but very unlike our priests in his dress. Thinking him a layman, the abbot, though inwardly calm, threatened him with a very ferocious voice, saying: "Come, perfidious old man, show me the most powerful relics you have, or you shall die immediately." The latter, terrified by the sound rather than the words, since he heard but did not understand what was said, and knowing that Martin could not speak Greek, began in the *Romana lingua*, of which he knew a little, to entreat Martin and by soft words to turn away the latter's wrath, which in truth did not exist. In reply, the abbot succeeded in getting out a few words of the same language, sufficient to make the old man understand what he wanted. The latter, observing Martin's face and dress, and thinking it more tolerable that a religious man should handle the sacred relics with fear and reverence, than that worldly men should, perchance, pollute them with their worldly hands, opened a chest bound with iron and showed the desired treasure, which was more grateful and pleasing to Martin than all the royal wealth of Greece. The abbot hastily and eagerly thrust in both hands and working quickly, filled with the fruits of the sacrilege both his own and his chaplain's bosom. He wisely concealed what seemed the most valuable and departed without opposition.

Moreover what and how worthy of veneration those relics which the holy robber appropriated were, is told more fully at the end of this work.[1] When he was hastening to his vessel, so stuffed full, if I may use the expression, those who knew and loved him, saw him from their ships as they were themselves hastening to the booty, and inquired joyfully whether he had stolen anything, or with what he was so loaded down as he walked. With a joyful countenance, as always, and with pleasant words he said: "We have done well." To which they replied: "Thanks be to God."

1. See pp. 20-21.

List of Relics Stolen by Abbot Martin (Gunther)

Therefore "Blessed be the Lord God, who only doeth wondrous things," who in His unspeakable kindness and mercy has looked upon and made glorious His church at Paris[1] through certain gifts of His grace, which he deigned to transmit to us through the venerable man, already so frequently mentioned, abbot Martin. In the presence of these the church exults and by their protection any soul faithful to God is aided and assisted. In order that the readers' trust in these may be strengthened, we have determined to give a partial list.

First, of the highest importance and worthy of all veneration: A trace of the blood of our Lord Jesus Christ, which was shed for the redemption of all mankind.

Second, a piece of the cross of our Lord on which the Son of the Father, the new Adam, sacrificed for us, paid the debt of the old Adam.

Third, a not inconsiderable piece of St. John, the forerunner of our Lord.

Fourth, the arm of St. James, the Apostle, whose memory is venerated by the whole church.

There were also relics of the other saints, whose names are as follows:

Christopher, the martyr.
George, the martyr.
Theodore, the martyr.
The foot of St. Cosmas, the martyr.
Part of the head of Cyprian, the martyr.
Pantaleon, the martyr.
A tooth of St. Lawrence.
Demetrius, the martyr.
Stephen, the proto-martyr.
Vincentius, Adjutus, Mauritius and his companions.
Crisantius and Darius, the martyrs.
Gervasius and Protasius, the martyrs.
Primus, the martyr.
Sergius and Bacchus, the martyrs.

1. In upper Elsass.

Protus, the martyr.

John and Paul, the martyrs.

Also relics from the following: the place of the Nativity of our Lord; Calvary; our Lord's sepulchre; the stone rolled away; the place of our Lord's ascension; the stone on which John stood when he baptized the Lord; the spot where Christ raised Lazarus; the stone on which Christ was presented in the temple; the stone on which Jacob slept; the stone where Christ fasted; the stone where Christ prayed; the table on which Christ ate the supper; the place where He was captured; the place where the mother of our Lord died; His grave; the grave of St. Peter, the apostle; the relics of the holy apostles, Andrew and Philip; the place where the Lord gave the law to Moses; the holy patriarchs, Abraham, Isaac and Jacob; St. Nicholas, the bishop; Adelasius, the bishop; Agricius, the bishop; John Chrysostom; John, the almsgiver; the milk of the mother of our Lord; Margaret, the virgin; Perpetua, the virgin; Agatha, the virgin; Agnes, the virgin; Lucia, the virgin; Cecilia, the virgin; Adelgundis and Euphemia, the virgins.

Written and sealed—in this year of our Lord's Incarnation, 1205, in the reign of Philip, king of the Romans, Innocent the supreme pontiff presiding over the holy Roman church—under the direction of the bishops Lutholdus of Basel and Henry of Strassburg.

2. Selections from the Letters of Pope Innocent III

The first of these two letters, written around May of 1205, shows the impact of the capture of Constantinople upon the pope who had planned the Crusade. The second shows how sharply Innocent realized the dangers which the conquest raised for the Holy Land—crusaders could be absolved of their vows, strength could be drawn off from Syria to Constantinople, and the savagery of western Latins could only further prolong the separation of the two halves of Christendom. Both letters illustrate Innocent's irritation at the conquest and his determination to make the best of a bad affair.

The first letter is from Munro, The Fourth Crusade, *the second from James A. Brundage,* The Crusades: A Documentary Survey *(Milwaukee, Wisc.: Marquette University Press, 1962), pp. 208-209, reprinted with permission.*

Crusaders to Stay at Constantinople (Pope Innocent III)

To all the clergy and people in the Christian army at Constantinople.

If the Lord had granted the desires of His humble servants sooner, and had transferred as He has now done, the empire of Constantinople from the Greeks to the Latins before the fall of the Holy Land, perhaps Christianity would not be weeping today over the desolation of the land of Jerusalem. Since, therefore, through the wonderful transference of this empire God has deigned to open to you a way to recover that land, and the detention of this may lead to the restoration of that, we advise and exhort you all, and we enjoin upon you for the remission of your sins, to remain for a year in Roumania, in order to strengthen the empire in its devotion to the Apostolic See and to us, and in order to retain it in the power of the Latins; and to give wise advice and efficient aid to Baldwin, our most beloved son in Christ, the illustrious emperor of Constantinople; unless, perchance, your presence in the Holy Land should be necessary before that time, in which case you ought to hasten to guard it before the year elapses.

The Crusade Endangers The Holy Land: Pope Innocent III reprimands a Papal Legate

To Peter, Cardinal Priest of the Title of St. Marcellus, Legate of the Apostolic See.

We were not a little astonished and disturbed to hear that you and our beloved son the Cardinal Priest of the Title of St. Praxida and Legate of the Apostolic See, in fear of the looming perils of the Holy Land, have left the province of Jerusalem (which, at this point is in such great need) and that you have gone by ship to Constantinople. And now we see that what we dreaded has occurred and what we feared has come to pass. . . . For you, who ought to have looked for help for the Holy Land, you who should have stirred up others, both by word and by example, to assist the Holy Land—on your own initiative you sailed to Greece, bringing in your footsteps not only the pilgrims, but even the natives of the Holy Land who came to Constantinople, following our venerable brother, the Archbishop of Tyre. When you had deserted it, the Holy Land remained destitute of men, void of strength. Because of you, its last state was worse than the first, for all its friends deserted with you nor was there any admirer to console it. . . . We ourselves were not a little agitated and, with reason, we acted against you, since you had fallen in with this counsel and because you had deserted the Land which the Lord consecrated by his presence, the land in which our King marvelously performed the mystery of our redemption. . . .

It was your duty to attend to the business of your legation and to give careful consideration, not to the capture of the Empire of Constantinople, but rather to the defense of what is left of the Holy Land and, with the Lord's leave, the restoration of what has been lost. We made you our representative and we sent you to gain, not temporal, but rather eternal riches. And for this purpose, our brethren provided adequately for your needs.

We have just heard and discovered from your letters that you have absolved from their pilgrimage vows and their crusading obligations all the Crusaders who have remained to defend Constantinople from last March to the present. It is impossible not to be moved against you, for you neither should nor could give any such absolution.

Whoever suggested such a thing to you and how did they ever lead your mind astray? . . .

How, indeed, is the Greek church to be brought back into ecclesiastical union and to a devotion for the Apostolic See when she has been beset with so many afflictions and persecutions that she sees in the Latins only an example of perdition and the works of darkness, so that she now, and with reason, detests the Latins more than dogs? As for those who were supposed to be seeking the ends of Jesus Christ, not their own ends, whose swords, which they were supposed to use against the pagans, are now dripping with Christian blood—they have spared neither age nor sex. They have committed incest, adultery, and fornication before the eyes of men. They have exposed both matrons and virgins, even those dedicated to God, to the sordid lusts of boys. Not satisfied with breaking open the imperial treasury and plundering the goods of princes and lesser men, they also laid their hands on the treasures of the churches and, what is more serious, on their very possessions. They have even ripped silver plates from the altars and have hacked them to pieces among themselves. They violated the holy places and have carried off crosses and relics. . . .

Furthermore, under what guise can we call upon the other Western peoples for aid to the Holy Land and assistance to the Empire of Constantinople? When the Crusaders, having given up the proposed pilgrimage, return absolved to their homes; when those who plundered the aforesaid Empire turn back and come home with their spoils, free of guilt; will not people then suspect that these things have happened, not because of the crime involved, but because of your deed? Let the Lord's word not be stifled in your mouth. Be not like a dumb dog, unable to bark. Rather, let them speak these things publicly, let them protest before everyone, so that the more they rebuke you before God and on God's account, the more they will find you simply negligent. As for the absolution of the Venetian people being falsely accepted, against ecclesiastical rules, we will not at present argue with you. . . .

II. Crusade and Council, 1208-1215

1. The Albigensian Crusade: From the Chronicle of Roger of Wendover

Roger of Wendover began to write his chronicle at St. Albans monastery in England around 1217 and continued to 1235, when he was succeeded by Matthew Paris. Roger was uniquely well informed and a sensible user of documentary evidence. His account of the Council and the events of the Albigensian Crusade reflect the point of view of a learned, uninvolved English cleric who had the power of organizing events and presenting a coherent narrative. The selections from Roger's chronicle in this volume are taken from J. A. Giles' translation in Bohn's Antiquarian Library, London, *1849, Volume II. The best discussion of Roger's work is that by V. H. Galbraith,* Roger Wendover and Matthew Paris *(Glasgow, 1944).*

The Albigensian Heresy and the Launching of the Crusade, 1208.

About that time the depravity of the heretics called Albigenses, who dwelt in Gascony, Arumnia, and Alby, gained such power in the parts about Toulouse, and in the kingdom of Arragon, that they not only practised their impieties in secret as was done elsewhere, but preached their erroneous doctrine openly, and induced the simple and weak-minded to conform to them. The Albigenses are so called from the city of Alba, where that doctrine is said to have taken its rise. At length their perversity set the anger of God so completely at defiance, that they published the books of their doctrines amongst the lower orders, before the very eyes of the bishops and priests, and disgraced the chalices and sacred vessels in disrespect of the body and blood of Christ. Pope Innocent was greatly grieved at hearing these things, and he immediately sent preachers into all the districts of the west, and enjoined to the chiefs and other Christian people as a remission of their sins, that they should take the sign of the cross for the extirpation of this plague, and, opposing themselves to such disasters, should protect the Christian people by force of arms; he also added, by authority of the apostolic see, that whoever undertook the business of overthrowing the heretics according to his injunction, should, like those who visited the Lord's sepulchre, be protected from all hostile attacks both in property and person. At this preaching such a multitude of crusaders assembled, as it is not to be credited could have assembled in our country.

Of the Movements of the Crusaders against the Albigenses

When therefore they were all assembled and prepared for battle, the archbishop of Narbonne, the legate of the apostolic see in this expedition, and the chiefs of the army, namely the duke of Burgundy, the count of Nevers, and the count de Montfort, struck their camp and marched to lay siege to the city of Beziers. But before they got to it the lords of some of the castles, having little confidence in themselves, fled at the sight of their army; the knights and others who were left in charge of the said castles, went boldly as good catholics and surrendered themselves with their property, as well as the castles to the army of the crusaders; and, on the eve of St. Mary Magdalen, they surrendered the noble castle of Cermaine to a monk, the lord of the castle, who also possessed several others of great strength, having taken to flight. They warned the citizens of Beziers, through the bishop of that city, under penalty of excommunication, to make choice of one out of two alternatives; either to deliver the heretics and their property into the hands of the crusaders, or else to send them away from amongst them, otherwise they would be excommunicated, and their blood be on their own heads.

The heretics and their allies scornfully refused to accede to this, and mutually swore to defend the city; and, when they had pledged their faith, they hoped to be able for a long time to sustain the assaults of the crusaders. After the city was laid siege to, on the feast of St. Mary Magdalen, the catholic barons considered how they could save those amongst them who were catholics, and made overtures for their liberation; but the rabble and low people, without waiting for the command or orders of the chiefs, made an assault on the city, and, to the astonishment of the Christians, when the cry to arms was raised, and the army of the faith was rushing in all directions to the assaults, those who were defending the walls inside threw out the book of the gospel from the city on them, blaspheming the name of the Lord, and deriding their assailants; "Behold," they said, "your law, we take no heed to it; yours it shall be." The soldiers of the faith, incensed by such blasphemy and provoked by their insults, in less than three hours' time crossed the fosse and scaled the walls, by the Lord's assistance. Thus was the city taken, and on the same day it was sacked and burnt, a great slaughter of the infidels taking place as the punishment of God; but, under his protection, very few of the catholics were slain. After the lapse of a few days, when the report of this miracle was spread abroad, the Lord scattered before the face of the crusaders, as it were without their assistance, those who had blasphemed his name and his law, and at length the followers of this heretical depravity were so alarmed that they fled to the recesses of the mountains, and what may be believed, they left more than a hundred untenanted castles, between Beziers and Carcassone, stocked with food and all kinds of stores, which they could not take with them in their flight.

The Capture of the City and Castle of Carcassone

The crusaders, moving their camp from this place, arrived on the feast of St. Peter "ad vincula" at Carcassone, a populous city, and till now glorying in its wickedness, abounding in riches, and well fortified. On the following day they made an assault, and within two or three hours they crossed the

entrenchments and scaled the walls amidst showers of missiles from the cross bows, and the blows of the lances and
swords of its wicked defenders. After this they set up their
engines of war, and on the eighth day the greater suburb was
taken after a great many of the enemy, who had incautiously
exposed themselves, were slain, and the suburbs of the city,
which seemed larger than the body of the town, were altogether destroyed. The enemy being thus confined in the
narrow streets of the city, and suffering as well from their
numbers as from want of provisions more than is credible,
offered themselves and all their property, together with the
city to the crusaders, on condition of their lives being preserved out of mercy, and of being saved for at least one day.
After holding a council, therefore, the barons received the
city almost as it were under compulsion; in the first place
because, in men's opinion, it was deemed impregnable; for
another reason because, if that city were altogether destroyed, there would not be found a nobleman of the army
who would undertake the government of that country, as
there would not be a place in the subdued land where he
could reside. Therefore, that the land, which the Lord had
delivered into the hands of his servants, might be preserved
to his honour and the advantage of Christianity, the noble
Simon de Montfort earl of Leicester was, by the common
consent of prelates and barons, chosen as ruler of that country; and into his hands was delivered as a prisoner the noble
Roger, formerly viscount and ruler of that country, together
with the whole of the province, including about a hundred
castles, which, within one month, the Lord designed to restore to the catholic unity; and amongst these same castles
were several of such strength that there would have been, in
the opinion of men, but little cause to fear any army. After
effecting this, the count of Nevers and a large part of the
army returned home, whilst the illustrious duke of Burgundy
and the rest of the nobles proceeded with their army to the
extirpation of this heretical depravity, and after this they
delivered into the hands of earl Simon de Montfort several
more castles which they took either by fair means or by
threats.

Messengers Sent to Toulouse by the Crusaders

As the city of Toulouse had been reported to have been long tainted with this pestiferous sin, the barons sent special messengers, namely, the archbishop of Santonge, the bishop of Foroli, the viscount of St. Florentius, and the lord Accald de Roussillon, to the inhabitants of that city with letters from them, ordering them to deliver up to the army of the crusaders the heretics of that city, and all their property. But if by chance they should say that they were not heretics; that those who were signified and expressed by name should come to them to make a plain declaration of their faith, according to Christian custom, before the whole army; and should they refuse to do this they would, by the same letters, excommunicate their chief officers and counsellors, and place the whole town of Toulouse with its dependencies under an interdict. In this year, on the fourteenth of October, Geoffrey Fitz-Peter, justiciary of England, closed his life.

The Destruction of Toulouse, 1226–1229

About the same time a crusade was preached throughout the French provinces in general by the Roman legate, that all who could carry arms, should assume the cross against the count of Toulouse and his followers, who were said to be infected with the foul stain of heresy. At his preaching, a great number of prelates as well as laity assumed the cross, being induced to do so more by fear of the French king or to obtain favour with the legate, than by their zeal for justice; for it seemed to many to be a sin to attack a true Christian, especially as all were aware that, at the council lately held at Bourges, the said count had with many entreaties begged of the legate to go to each one of the cities in his territory to inquire into the articles of their faith, and had declared that if he, the legate, should find the inhabitants of any city to hold opinions contrary to the catholic faith, he himself would exact full satisfaction from them; and if he found any city in a state of disobedience, he would, as far as lay in his power, compel that city and its inhabitants to make atonement; and

as for himself he offered, if he had sinned in any way, which
he did not remember to have done, to give full satisfaction
to God and the holy church, as a faithful Christian; and if the
legate wished it, he would undergo a trial of his faith. All
these offers the legate refused, nor could this catholic count
find any favour with him without abandoning and forswear-
ing his inheritance for himself and his heirs after him. The
French king at the preaching of this legate assumed the
cross, but would not proceed in this expedition unless he first
obtained letters from the pope to the king of England, forbidding him, under penalty of excommunication, to annoy him
the French king, or to make war against him concerning any
territory he at present held, whether justly or unjustly, as
long as he was engaged in the service of the pope and the
church of Rome, in exterminating the heretic Albigenses,
and their abettor and accomplice the count of Toulouse, but
should aid him with assistance and advice in forwarding the
cause of the faith. After this the French king and the legate
appointed our Lord's ascension-day for all those who had
assumed the cross to assemble, under penalty of excommunication, at Lyons, equipped with horses and arms, to follow
them on the proposed expedition.

Of the Siege of Avignon by Louis the French King

In the meantime our Lord's ascension arrived, on which
day all the French crusaders had been ordered by the king
and the legate to assemble without fail. The king, having
made all the necessary preparations for the expedition at
Lyons, proceeded on his journey with, as it seemed, an invin-
cible army, followed by the legate, the archbishops, bishops,
and other prelates of the churches; the army was computed
to consist of about fifty thousand knights and horse-soldiers,
besides foot-soldiers, who could hardly be counted. The legate then publicly excommunicated the count of Toulouse
and all his abettors, and laid all his territory under an interdict. The king, as we have said, set out with shields and
standards glittering, and his march was so awful that it looked
like an army of castles in motion, and at length entered the

province of the count of Toulouse. On the eve of Whit-Sunday they all reached Avignon, which was the first city in the count's dominion that they came to, and they determined to commence their attacks there, and thus to subdue the whole of the count's territory with the inhabitants of it from beginning to end. The king and the legate on their arrival there deceitfully asked leave of the inhabitants to pass through the city, saying that they had come thither with peaceable intentions, and asked a passage through the city only to make a short cut in their march. The citizens, however, after deliberating on this request, put no faith in their assertions, and said that they wanted to get into the city with treacherous intentions rather than to make a short cut. The king then becoming enraged, swore that he would not leave the spot till he had taken the city, and immediately ordered his engines to be arranged round the place and a fierce assault to be made. A severe attack was then commenced, and petrariae, cross-bows, and all other kinds of military weapons were now put in constant use. On the other hand the city, till that time unattempted by hostile troops, was well defended by trenches, walls, turrets, and ramparts outside, whilst within it was well garrisoned with knights and thousands of soldiers, and well supplied with horses, arms, collections of stones for missiles, engines and barriers, and was well stored with provisions, and did not therefore fear the assaults of the besiegers; for the defenders of the city bravely hurled on them stone for stone, weapon for weapon, spear for spear, and dart for dart, inflicting deadly wounds on the besieging French.

Of the Mortality and Famine amongst the Besiegers

After the siege had been carried on for a length of time, the provisions of the besiegers failed them and numbers of the troops died; for the count of Toulouse, like a skilful soldier, had, before the arrival of the French, removed out of their way all kinds of provisions, together with the old men, women, children, and the horses and cattle, so that they were deprived of all kinds of sustenance. And it was not only the

men who suffered, but also the horses and cattle of the army
perished of hunger; for the count had caused all the fields
throughout the district to be ploughed up, so that there was
no supply of fodder for the cattle except what had been
brought from the French provinces; therefore large bodies
of troops were obliged to leave the camp to seek for provisions for the men and food for the horses, and on these excur-
sions they took many towns which opposed them, and they
often suffered great loss from attacks by the count of Toulouse, who with his troops lay in ambuscade for them. At this
siege the French were exposed to death in many ways, from
the mortality which was raging dreadfully amongst their
men and horses, from the deadly weapons and destructive
stones of the besieged who bravely defended the city, and
from the general famine which raged principally amongst
the poorer classes, who had neither food or money. In addition to the other miseries, which assailed the army without
intermission, there arose from the corpses of the men and
horses, which were dying in all directions, a number of large
black flies, which made their way inside the tents, pavilions,
and awnings, and affected the provisions and liquor; and
being unable to drive them away from their cups and plates,
they caused sudden death amongst them. The king and the
legate were in dismay, for if such a great and powerful expedition were to return, with their purpose unaccomplished,
the French as well as the Romans would incur much taunt-
ing. The chiefs of the army, then, to whom the delay seemed
long on account of such numbers of deaths, begged the inferior ranks as well as their chiefs to attack the city; on this
such a multitude of troops marched against the city, that, in
marching over a bridge which was built over the Rhone, the
bridge was broken, either by the citizens, or by the weight
of the troops who were fighting there, and about three thousand men were precipitated into the rapid stream. Then
there arose a cry of exultation from the citizens, but dismay
and confusion pervaded the French army. After this the citizens, watching their opportunity, sallied from the city one
day in great force when the French were sitting at table
eating and drinking, and rushing on them when unprepared

for them, slew two thousand of the French, and then returned into the city without loss to themselves, and these sallies they continually made against them. The French king was in dismay, and ordered the slain to be thrown into the Rhone, to avoid the stench, for with such a number of dead bodies they had no other burial place. They then made a wide deep trench between them and the city, and the operations of the siege were carried on at a greater distance from it. The legate and the whole assembly of prelates during this time, having no other means of punishment, excommunicated the count of Toulouse, the citizens, and all the inhabitants of the province.

The Death of Louis the French King

At this time Louis king of the French, to escape the pestilence which was committing great ravages in the camp, retired to a monastery called Montpensier, near the besieged town, to await the capture of the city; at that place Henry count of Champagne came to him, having been employed forty days in the siege, and, according to the French custom, asked leave to return home, and on the king's refusing his permission, he said that having served his forty days of duty he was not bound to, nor would he, stay any longer. The king then, roused to anger, declared with an oath, that if the count went away in this way he would ravage his territory with fire and sword. The count then, as report goes, being in love with his queen, caused some poison to be administered to the king, and being urged on by the impulses of desire he could not abide longer delay. After the departure of the count, as he had said he would, the king was taken dangerously ill, and, the poison working its way to his vitals, he was reduced to the point of death; some however assert that he died not by poison but of dysentery. On the death of the king, Roman the legate of the apostolic see, who was present at the siege, and the prelates his secret advisers, who were also there, concealed the death of the king until the city should be surrendered; for if the siege were to be now raised, a great reproach would be cast on them. The legate and the prelates, therefore, who were at the siege, pretended that the king was detained by severe illness, but said that in the opinion of his physicians he would soon be convalescent, and then exhorted the chiefs of the different battalions to attack the city with all their power. They preserved the king's body with large quantities of salt, and, burying his entrails in the convent, they ordered his body to be wrapped in waxed linen and bulls' hides; it was then placed in safe custody in the convent, and the legate and the prelates then returned to the siege. However finding that they gained no advantage, but were entirely failing owing to different misfortunes, the legate, by the advice of the elders in the camp, sent a message into the city asking them, on receipt of security, for safe conduct to and from the city, to send twelve of the elders of the city to the legate as soon as possible to make terms of peace.

How the City of Avignon Was Taken by the French by Treachery

After hostages had been given for their safety, twelve citizens came out to a conference with the legate, when, after a long discussion about peace, he earnestly advised the citizens to surrender themselves saving their persons, their property and possessions, and all their liberties, to the utmost extent that they had ever enjoyed them. To this the messengers replied, that they would on no account surrender themselves to live under the dominion of the French, whose pride and fierce insolence they had often experienced. After much disputing on both sides, the legate at length asked permission to go into the city with the prelates who were present, to put the faith of the inhabitants to the test, declaring on oath that he had prolonged the siege only to provide for the safety of their souls; he also added, that the cry of infidelity, which had gained power in the city, had reached the pope, and he therefore desired to know whether they supported this cry by their actions. The citizens then, trusting to the promises of the legate, and having no suspicions of treachery, after an oath had been taken on both sides, on the above-named condition, gave permission to the legate and the prelates to enter the city without any others, and in company with them. But, as had been pre-arranged, as soon as the gates were open, the French treacherously, and in disgraceful disregard of the oath which had been made by the legate, forced their way into the city and made prisoners of the inhabitants, and having thus treacherously gained a victory they destroyed the towers and walls of this noble place. The legate then consigned the city to the charge of the French, and raising the siege he ordered the body of the king to be carried to Paris by the priests assembled, to be buried amongst his ancestors as was the custom with kings. The king died, as they say, in the month of September, but they concealed his death for a month or more. Of those who went to the siege with the king, twenty-two thousand died at the place, including those who were slain and drowned, as well as those who died of the pestilence or by natural death, and thus left great cause of tears and sorrow to their wives and children; hence it seems clearly evident that an unjust war had been undertaken, of which covetousness was the cause rather than the wish to exterminate heresy.

2. The Children's Crusade: From the Chronicle of the City of Cologne and from the Chronicle of Matthew Paris

The following two selections offer divergent views of one of the most remarkable aspects of Crusade history, the Children's Crusade of 1212–1213. Like the followers of Peter the Hermit in 1096, those youths who, apparently spontaneously, marched from France and Germany to the Mediterranean in the hope that God would deliver the Moslems into their hands were captured, turned back, sold as slaves, or killed by the men into whose hands they fell. The incident has a ghastly character, but many who witnessed the events of this movement were profoundly touched by the children's efforts.

One of these was Pope Innocent III himself. Matthew Paris, as the second selection shows, held no such respect. The first selection here is from The Chronicle of the City of Cologne, *translated by James A. Brundage, in* The Crusades: A Documentary Survey, *Marquette University Press. Reprinted with permission.*

In this year occurred an outstanding thing and one much to be marveled at, for it is unheard of throughout the ages. About the time of Easter and Pentecost, without anyone having preached or called for it and prompted by I know not what spirit, many thousands of boys, ranging in age from six years to full maturity, left the plows or carts which they were driving, the flocks which they were pasturing, and anything else which they were doing. This they did despite the wishes of their parents, relatives, and friends who sought to make them draw back. Suddenly one ran after another to take the cross. Thus, by groups of twenty, or fifty, or a hundred, they put up banners and began to journey to Jerusalem. They were asked by many people on whose advice or at whose urging they had set out upon this path. They were asked especially since only a few years ago many kings, a great many dukes, and innumerable people in powerful companies had gone there and had returned with the business unfinished. The present groups, moreover, were still of tender years and were neither strong enough nor powerful enough to do anything. Everyone, therefore, accounted them foolish and imprudent for trying to do this. They briefly replied that they were equal to the Divine will in this matter and that, whatever God might wish to do with them, they would accept it willingly and with humble spirit. They thus made some little progress on their journey. Some were turned back at Metz, others at Piacenza, and others even at Rome. Still others got to Marseilles, but whether they crossed to the Holy Land or what their end was is uncertain. One thing is sure: that of the many thousands who rose up, only very few returned.

The translation below is from Roger of Wendover's Chronicle in Bohn's Antiquarian Library, *vol. II, p. 282.*

Matthew Paris

In the course of the same year, during the following summer, there sprang up in France a false doctrine never before heard of: for a certain youth, who was a boy in age, but of vile habits, at the instigation of the devil, went about amongst the cities and castles of France, chanting in French these words: "O Lord Jesus Christ, restore to us the holy cross!" with many other additions. And when the rest of the boys of his own age saw and heard him, they followed him in endless numbers, and, being infatuated by the wiles of the devil, they left their fathers and mothers, nurses, and all their friends, singing in the same way as their teacher; and, what was astonishing, no lock could detain them, nor could the persuasions of their parents recall them, but they followed their said master towards the Mediterranean sea, and, crossing it, they marched on in procession singing. No city could hold them on account of numbers; their leader was placed in a car ornamented with a canopy, and was attended by armed guards raising their shouts around him. They were so numerous that they squeezed one another together, and that one thought himself happy who could gain a thread or a shred of his garment. But at last, their old enemy Satan plotted against them, and they all perished either on land or by sea.

3. The Fourth Lateran Council, 1215: From the Chronicle of Roger of Wendover

The Fourth Lateran Council of 1215 was one of the great events of the early thirteenth century. It drew to a close the work of the great legislative councils of the twelfth century, imposed papal supremacy, and prepared the way for a full-dress crusade in the following years. Besides the references cited in the Introduction, see also S. Kuttner and A. García y García, "A New Eyewitness Account of the Fourth Lateran Council," Traditio *20 (1964), 115–178, and J. W. Baldwin,* Masters, Princes, and Merchants: The Social Views of Peter the Chanter and His Circle (*Princeton, 1970*), *Vol. I, pp. 315–343.*

Of the General Council Held by Pope Innocent at Rome

In the same year, namely, A.D. 1215, a sacred and general synod was held in the month of November, in the church of the Holy Saviour at Rome, called Constantian, at which our lord pope Innocent, in the eighteenth year of his pontificate, presided, and which was attended by four hundred and twelve bishops. Amongst the principal of these were the two patriarchs of Constantinople and Jerusalem. The patriarch of Antioch could not come, being detained by serious illness, but he sent his vicar, the bishop of Antaradus; the patriarch of Alexandria being under the dominion of the Saracens, did the best he could, sending a deacon his cousin in his place. There were seventy-seven primates and metropolitans present, more than eight hundred abbots and priors; and of the proxies of archbishops, bishops, abbots, priors, and chapters, who were absent, the number is not known. There was also present a great multitude of ambassadors from the emperor of Constantinople, the king of Sicily, who was elected emperor of Rome, the kings of France, England, Hungary, Jerusalem, Cyprus, Arragon, and other princes and nobles, and from cities and other places. When all of these were assembled in the place above-mentioned, and, according to the custom of general councils, each was placed according to his rank, the pope himself first delivered an exhortation, and then the sixty articles were recited in full council, which seemed agreeable to some and tedious to others. At length he commenced to preach concerning the business of the cross, and the subjection of the Holy Land, adding as follows: "Moreover, that nothing be omitted in the matter of the cross of Christ, it is our will and command, that patriarchs, archbishops, bishops, abbots, priors, and others, who have the charge of spiritual matters, carefully set forth the work of the cross to the people entrusted to their care; and in the name of the Father, the Son, and the Holy Ghost, the one alone and eternal God, supplicate kings, dukes, princes, marquises, earls, barons, and other nobles, and also the communities of cities, towns, and villages, if they cannot go in person to the assistance of the Holy Land, to furnish a suitable number of soldiers, with all supplies necessary for three years, according to their means, in remission of their sins, as in the general letters is expressed; and it is also our will that those who build ships for this purpose be partakers in this remission. But to those who refuse, if any be so ungrateful, let it be on our behalf declared, that they will for a certainty account to us for this at the awful judgment of a rigorous Judge; considering, before they do refuse, with what chance of salvation they will be able to appear before the only God and the only-begotten Son of God, to whose hands the Father has entrusted all things, if they refuse to serve that crucified one, in this their proper service, by whose gift they hold life, by whose kindness they are supported, and by whose blood they have been redeemed. And we, wishing to set an example to others, give and grant thirty thousand pounds for this business, besides a fleet, which we will supply to those who assume the cross from this city and the neighbouring districts; and we moreover assign for the accomplishment of this, three thousand marks of silver, which remain to us out of the alms of some of the true faith. And as we desire to have the other prelates of the churches, and also the clergy in general, as partakers both in the merit and the reward, it is our decree, that all of them, both people and pastors, shall contribute for the assistance of the Holy Land the twentieth portion of their ecclesiastical profits for three years, except those who have assumed the cross or are about to assume it and set out for the Holy Land in person; and we and our brethren the cardinals of the holy church of Rome will pay a full tenth part of ours. It is also our order that all clerks or laymen, after assuming the cross, shall remain secure under our protection and that of St. Peter; and also under the protection of the archbishops, bishops, and all the prelates of God's church, and that all their property shall be so arranged, as to remain untouched and undisturbed until certain information is obtained of their death or their return. And if any of those who go on this crusade are bound by oath to the payment of usury, their creditors shall by ecclesiastic authority be compelled to forgive them their oath and to desist from exacting their usury; and we make the same decree with regard to the Jews by the secular authority, that they may be induced to do this. Moreover be it known, that the prelates of churches, who are careless in granting justice to crusaders, or their proxies, or their families, will meet with severe punishment. Moreover, by the advice of wise men, we determine that those who thus assume the cross, shall prepare themselves so as to assemble on the first of June next ensuing, and those who determine to cross by sea will assemble in the kingdom of Sicily, some at Brundusium, and others at Messina, at which place we also have determined, under God's favour, to be present, that by our assistance and counsel the Christian army may be duly regulated, and may set out with the blessing of God and the apostolic see. And we, trusting to the mercy of the omnipotent God, and to the authority of the blessed apostles Peter and Paul, by virtue of that power which the Lord has granted to us, unworthy though we are, of binding and loosing, grant to all who shall undertake this business in person and at their own expense, full pardon for their sins, for which they shall be truly contrite in heart, and of which they shall have made confession, and in the rewarding of the just we promise an increase of eternal salvation; and to those who do not come in person, out at their own expense send suitable persons according to their means, and also to those who come in person though at the expense of others, we likewise grant full pardon for their sins. And it is also our will that those should share in this forgiveness who out of their own property shall furnish proper supplies for the assistance of the said country, or who have rendered seasonable counsel and assistance on the aforesaid matters. And for all those who proceed on this expedition the holy and universal synod bestows the favour of its prayers and good wishes, to the end that they may better obtain eternal salvation. Amen."

4. The Crusading Privilege of Innocent III, given at the Fourth Lateran Council, 1215

Translation from E. F. Henderson, Select Historical Documents of the Middle Ages (London and New York, 1896), pp. 337–344.

Aspiring with ardent desire to liberate the Holy Land from the hands of the ungodly, by the counsel of prudent men who fully know the circumstances of times and places, the holy council approving: we decree that the crusaders shall so prepare themselves that, at the Calends of the June following the next one, all who have arranged to cross by sea shall come together in the kingdom of Sicily; some, as shall be convenient and fitting, at Brindisi, and others at Messina and the places adjoining on both sides; where we also have arranged then to be present in person if God wills it, in order that by our counsel and aid the Christian army may be healthfully arranged, about to start with the divine and apostolic benediction.

1. Against the same term, also, those who have decided to go by land shall endeavour to make themselves ready; announcing to us, in the meantime, this determination, so that we may grant them, for counsel and aid, a suitable legate from our side.

2. Priests, moreover, and other clergy who shall be in the Christian army, subordinates as well as prelates, shall diligently insist with prayer and exhortation, teaching the crusaders by word and example alike that they should always have the divine fear and love before their eyes, and that they should not say or do anything which might offend the divine majesty. Although at times they may lapse into sin, through true penitence they shall soon arise again; showing humility of heart and body, and observing moderation as well in their living as in their apparel; altogether avoiding dissensions and emulations; rancour and spleen being entirely removed from them. So that, thus armed with spiritual and material weapons, they may fight the more securely against the enemies of

the faith; not presuming in their own power, but hoping in the divine virtue.

3. To the clergy themselves, moreover, we grant that they may retain their benefices intact for three years, as if they were residing in their churches; and, if it shall be necessary, they may be allowed to place them in pledge for that time.

4. Lest therefore this holy undertaking should happen to be impeded or retarded, we distinctly enjoin on all the prelates of the churches, that, separately, throughout their districts, they diligently move and induce to fulfil their vows to God those who have arranged to resume the sign of the cross; and besides these, the others who are signed with the cross, and who have hitherto been signed; and that, if it shall be necessary, through sentences of excommunication against their persons and of interdict against their lands, all backsliding being put an end to, they compel them to fulfil their vows: those only being excepted who shall meet with some impediment on account of which, according to the ordinance of the apostolic chair, their vow may rightly be commuted or deferred.

5. Besides this, lest anything which pertains to the work of Jesus Christ be omitted, we will and command that the patriarchs, archbishops, bishops, abbots and others who obtain the care of souls shall studiously propound to those committed to them the word of the cross, exhorting through the Father and the Son and the Holy Spirit—the one sole true eternal God—the kings, dukes, princes, margraves, counts and barons and other magnates, also the communities of the cities towns and burghs, that those who do not in person go to the aid of the Holy Land, shall donate a suitable number of warriors, with the necessary expenses for three years, according to their own wealth, for the remission of their sins, —as has been expressed in our general letters, and as, for the greater safety, we shall also express below. Of this remission we wish to be partakers not only those who furnish their own ships, but also those who on account of this work have striven to build new ships.

6. To those that refuse, moreover, if any by chance shall be so ungrateful to our Lord God, they (the clergy) shall

firmly protest on behalf of the apostolic see, that they shall know that for this they are about to answer to us, at the final day of a strict investigation, before the tremendous Judgment. First considering, however, with what conscience or with what security they will be able to confess in the presence of Jesus Christ the only begotten Son of God, into whose hands the Father gave all things, if they shall refuse in this matter, as if it were properly their own, to serve Him who was crucified for sinners; by whose gift they live, by whose benefit they are sustained, nay, more, by whose blood they are redeemed.

7. Lest, however, we seem to impose upon the shoulders of men heavy and unbearable burdens which we are unwilling to put a finger to, like those who only say, and do not do; behold we, from what we have been able to spare beyond our necessary and moderate expenses, do grant and give thirty thousand pounds to this work; and, besides the transport from Rome and the neighbouring places that we have granted, we assign in addition, for this same purpose, three thousand marks of silver which have remained over to us from the alms of some of the faithful; the rest having been faithfully distributed for the needs and uses of the aforesaid Land, through the hand of the abbot of blessed memory, the patriarch of Jerusalem, and the masters of the Templars and Hospitallers.

8. Desiring, moreover, to have the other prelates of the churches, as well as the whole clergy, as participators and sharers both in the merit and in the reward, we have decreed with the general approbation of the council, that absolutely the entire clergy, subordinates as well as prelates, shall give the twentieth part of their ecclesiastical revenues for three years in aid of the Holy Land, through the hands of those who shall by the care of the pope be appointed for this purpose; certain monks alone being excepted, who are rightly to be exempted from this taxation; likewise those who, having assumed or being about to assume the cross, are on the point of making the expedition.

9. We, also, and our brothers the cardinals of the holy Roman Church, shall pay fully one tenth; and they shall all

know that they are all bound to faithfully observe this under penalty of excommunication; so that those who in this matter shall knowingly commit fraud shall incur sentence of excommunication.

10. Since, indeed, those who with right judgment remain in the service of the divine Commander ought to rejoice in a special privilege: when the time of the expedition exceeds one year in length the crusaders shall be free from taxes and talliages and other burdens. Upon their assuming the cross we take their persons and goods under the protection of the blessed Peter and of ourselves, so that they shall remain under the care of the archbishops, bishops and other prelates of the church. Special protectors, nevertheless, being deputed for this purpose, so that, until most certain news shall have been obtained either of their death or of their return, their possessions shall remain intact and unassailed. And if any one presume to the contrary he shall be restrained by ecclesiastical censure.

11. But if any of those proceeding thither are bound by an oath to pay interest, we command, under the same penalty, that their creditors be compelled to remit the oath given them and to desist from claiming interest. But if any one of their creditors shall compel them to pay interest, we command that, by a similar process, they shall be compelled to restore it. But we command that Jews shall be compelled by the secular power to remit their interst; and, until they shall remit it, all intercourse with them on the part of all the followers of Christ shall be denied, under pain of excommunication. For those, moreover, who are unable at present to pay their debts to the Jews, the secular princes shall so provide, with useful delay, that, from the time when they started on their journey until most certain news is obtained of their death or of their return, they shall not incur the inconvenience of interest. The Jews being compelled to count the income which they in the meantime received from the lands pledged to them, towards the principal of the sum loaned, the necessary expenses being deducted; for such a benefice does not suffer much loss, when it so delays the payment that it is not itself absorbed by the debt. The prel-

ates of the churches, indeed, who shall be found negligent in rendering justice to the crusaders and their families, shall know that they shall be severely punished.

12. Furthermore, since corsairs and pirates excessively impede the aiding of the Holy Land, taking and despoiling those who go to and return from it, we bind with the chain of the anathema their especial aiders and favourers. Forbidding, under threat of the anathema, that any one make common cause with them through any contract of buying or selling; and enjoining on the rectors of their cities and districts to recall and restrain them from this iniquity. Otherwise, since to be unwilling to disturb the wicked is nothing else than to foster them, and since he is not without suspicion of secret collusion who desists from opposing a manifest crime: we will and command that, against their persons and lands, ecclesiastical severity shall be exercised by the prelates of the churches.

13. Moreover we excommunicate and anathematize those false and impious Christians who, against Christ Himself and the Christian people, carry arms, iron, and wood for ships to the Saracens. Those also who sell to them galleys or ships and who, in the pirate ships of the Saracens, keep watch or do the steering, or give them any aid, counsel or favour with regard to their war machines or to any thing else, to the harm of the Holy Land;—we decree shall be punished with the loss of their own possessions and shall be the slaves of those who capture them. And we command that on Sundays and feast days, throughout all the maritime cities, this sentence shall be renewed; and to such the lap of the church shall not be opened unless they shall send all that they have received from such damnable gains, and as much more of their own as aid to the aforesaid Land; so that they may be punished with a penalty equal to the amount of their original fault. But if by chance they be insolvent, those guilty of such things shall be otherwise punished; that through their punishment others may be prevented from having the audacity to presume to act similarly.

14. We prohibit, moreover, all Christians, and under pain of anathema, interdict them from sending across or taking

across their ships to the lands of the Saracens who inhabit the oriental districts, until four years are past; so that, in this way, greater means of transport may be prepared for those wishing to cross to the aid of the Holy Land, and the aforesaid Saracens may be deprived of the by no means small advantage which has, as a rule, accrued to them from this.

15. Although, indeed, in different councils, tournaments have been generally forbidden under penalty: inasmuch as at this time the matter of the crusade is very much impeded by them, we, under pain of excommunication, do firmly forbid them to be carried on for the next three years.

16. Since, moreover, in order to carry on this matter it is most necessary that the princes and the people of Christ should mutually observe peace, the holy universal synod urging us: we do establish that, at least for four years, throughout the whole Christian world, a general peace shall be observed; so that, through the prelates of the churches, the contending parties may be brought back to inviolably observe a full peace or a firm truce. And those who, by chance, shall scorn to acquiesce, shall be most sternly compelled to do so through excommunication against their persons, and interdict against their land; unless the maliciousness of the injuries shall be so great, that the persons themselves ought not to have the benefit of such peace. But if by chance they despise the ecclesiastical censure, not without reason shall they fear lest, through the authority of the church, the secular power may be brought to bear against them as against disturbers of what pertains to the Crucified One.

17. We therefore, trusting in the mercy of almighty God and in the authority of the blessed apostles Peter and Paul, from that power of binding and loosing which God conferred on us, although unworthy, do grant to all who shall undergo this labour in their own persons and at their own expense, full pardon of their sins of which in their heart they shall have freely repented, and which they shall have confessed; and, at the retribution of the just, we promise them an increase of eternal salvation. To those, moreover, who do not go thither in their own persons, but who only at their own expense, according to their wealth and quality, send suitable men; and

to those likewise who, although at another's expense, go, nevertheless, in their own persons: we grant full pardon of their sins. Of this remission, also, we will and grant that, according to the quality of their aid and the depth of their devotion, all shall be partakers who shall suitably minister from their goods towards the aid of that same Land, or who shall give timely counsel and aid. To all, moreover, who piously proceed in this work the general synod imparts in common the aid of all its benefits, that it may worthily help them to salvation.

Given at the Lateran, on the nineteenth day before the Calends of January (Dec. 14th), in the eighteenth year of our pontificate.

III. The Fifth Crusade, 1217-1222

1. Signs and Portents: From the Chronicle of Roger of Wendover

The Crusade invoked by the Fourth Lateran Council began to move in 1217. These brief selections offer a flavor of men's apprehensiveness and eagerness to answer Pope Innocent's summons.

Of Signs in the Heavens by which the Province of Cologne Was Incited to Assist in the Crusade, 1217

In the month of May in this year, on the sixth day before Whitsuntide, the province of Cologne was awakened to its duty to the Saviour; for at the town of Bebon in Friesland there appeared in the sky the form of the cross in three places, one towards the north of a white colour, another towards the south of the same form and colour, and the third in the middle of a dark colour, with the form of the crucifix, and the figure of a man suspended on it, with uplifted and extended arms, with nails driven through the feet and hands, and with the head bent down; this one was in the middle between the two others, on which latter did not appear the image of a human body; at another time and place too, namely, at a town of Friesland called Fuserhuse, there appeared near the sun a cross of a blue colour, and more people saw this than those who had seen the former crosses: a third cross appeared at the town of Doctham, where saint Bonifacius was crowned with martyrdom; at this place on the feast of the said martyr, many thousand men having collected together, a large white cross was visible, as though two planks were placed artificially across one another; this cross moved gradually from the north towards the east, and many thousands saw it.

How the Inhabitants of Cologne and Friesland Prepared to March to the Holy Land, 1218

About that time there was a great movement of the brave and warlike men in the provinces of Cologne and Friesland, for since the commencement of the preaching of the crusade after the general council, they had with great eagerness built three hundred ships and having embarked in them, to fulfil to the Lord their vows of pilgrimage, they set sail, and the greater part of them, with a large array of soldiers, had arrived at Lisbon, where a disagreement arose amongst them about laying siege to a strong castle called Alchatia, some being anxious to proceed, and others wishing to winter where they were; so the fleet was divided, and one part of it wintered at Gaeta and Sorrento, and the other part under the command of two chiefs, namely, William duke of Holland, and George count of Weise, laid siege to Alchacia. Whilst they were still employed in the siege, a large force of Saracens was assembled against them, but the Christians bravely gave them battle, and, by the divine assistance, conquered the infidels. One king amongst the pagans was slain, and numbers of others were killed and made prisoners; the castle was at last taken by the Germans, and held by the Christians.

2. The Capture of Damietta, by Oliver of Paderborn, translated with notes by Joseph J. Gavigan

Oliver's chronicle, written while he was on the Fifth Crusade during the years 1217–1222, is a complete eyewitness account of the response of Christendom to the crusading pleas of Pope Innocent III. It marks a major shift in Crusade strategy, since it was aimed at Egypt instead of Syria, and its near-success reflects the soundness of the change in tactics. The translation and notes printed here were first published in the University of Pennsylvania Translations and Reprints from the Original Sources of European History, Third Series, Volume II (Philadelphia, 1948). The entire work, except for the editorial apparatus, is reprinted below.

Here begins the history of Damietta whereat Master Oliver, compiler of this work and preacher of the Holy Cross, was undoubtedly present.

Foreword

"Let Mount Sion rejoice, and let the daughters of Juda be glad because of Thy judgments, O Lord. Sing ye to the Lord for He hath done great things";[1] writing and preaching, let them announce the wonders of the Lord[2] Who hath commanded His sanctified ones and hath called His strong ones in His wrath, them that exult not in their own strength, "not in the works of justice which they themselves have done,"[3] but in the glory of His majesty, Who is blessed in all things in eternity. For "the land whence arose the bread that came down from heaven"[4] in the place of His birth has been cut off by the sword, and by many fortifications which perfidious men occupy; "the stones of this land are the place of sapphires"[5] because it was the possession of the patriarchs, the nursling of the prophets, the teacher of the apostles, the mother of faith. "The clods of it are gold,"[6] because the guardians of religion have clung together by charity and

1. Psalms 47:12. All quotations from the Old Testament are made as closely as possible according to the Douay Version. Those from the New Testament are modeled upon the edition of the Confraternity of Christian Doctrine, Paterson, 1941.
2. Isaias 13:3.
3. Titus 3:5.
4. Romans 1:25; Job 28:5; John 6:33.
5. Job 28:6.
6. Job 28:6.

have never failed therein. Freed at last after many groans and frequent sighs, it now exults in hope; and trusting in goodness of its deliverer, rejoicing, it will rejoice when "the rod of sinners has been taken away from the lot of the just."[7] Indeed what we have seen and heard and have truly understood, we write to all who are orthodox without any admixture of falsity, so that whatever merit there is may appear to the praise of God, and in gratitude to Him.

Chapter 1

In the year 1217, when the truce of the Christians and Saracens[1] had expired, in the first general passage after the Lateran Council,[2] a large army of the Lord assembled in Acre, with the three kings of Jerusalem,[3] Hungary,[4] and Cyprus,[5] who, not bearing with them the mystic gifts, offered one not at all worthy of memory. The Duke of Austria[6] was there, and

7. Psalms 124:3.

1. The truce which expired in 1217 was one made with Saphadin by either Aymeri de Lusignan or John d'Ibelin when Regent of Jerusalem.

2. The Fourth Lateran Council (the twelfth oecumenical) of 1215, was the greatest of the Middle Ages and is sometimes referred to simply as *the* Lateran Council. It was summoned by Pope Innocent III (+1216). It defined the Incarnation and other mysteries against the Albigensians; condemned the errors of Joachim on the Trinity; recognized the second place of the Patriarch of Constantinople; forbade the establishment of new religious orders; legislated against pluralism; and stated the requirement of at least annual confession and communion.

3. John of Brienne, King of Jerusalem, 1210-25; Emperor of Constantinople, 1228-37. He received the crown of Jerusalem when he married Marie de Montferrat in 1210 and lost it in 1225 when his daughter Isabelle married Frederick II. He was military leader and hero of the expedition against Damietta but was absent for a time owing to his difficulties with Pelagius, and while he was advancing claims to the throne of Armenia.

4. Andrew II, King of Hungary, 1203-35, son of Bela III and Margaret, Princess of France. He left the crusade at the beginning of 1218. Later (1233) he became the husband of Yolanda Courtenay, Empress of Constantinople.

5. Hugh of Lusignan, King of Cyprus, 1205-18, son of Aymeri and Eschive d'Ibelin. He married Alice of Champagne-Jerusalem, daughter of Isabelle of Jerusalem and Henry of Champagne, who, after Hugh's death, played an important role in the politics of the Latin states.

6. Leopold VI, the Glorious, Duke of Austria, 1198-1230, who fought in Spain in 1212, but arrived too late for the famous battle of Las Navas de Tolosa.

the Duke of Meran[7] with many companions and men of noble birth, and the great soldiery of the Teutonic king. There were present pilgrim bishops, the Archbishop of Nicosia,[8] Raab,[9] Erlau,[10] Hungary,[11] Bayeux,[12] Bamberg,[13] Zeitz,[14] Münster,[15] and Utrecht;[16] with them was a powerful and noble man, Lord Walter of Avesnes,[17] who, returning in the spring crossing, left forty soldiers in the service of the Holy Land, and provided them with funds sufficient for a year. The Bavarians conducted themselves insolently, and contrary to the law of pilgrims, by destroying the gardens and orchards of the Christians, even casting religious out of their hospices; when this did not satisfy them, they killed the Christians. The Duke of Austria, like a Catholic prince, fought for Christ throughout.

7. Otto VII, duke of Meran, 1204-34, belonged to a particularly illustrious family. His parents were Berthold IV, Duke of Meran (+1204), and Agnes of Groitsch-Rochlitz (+1194 or 1195). Otto married Beatrice of Hohenstaufen, Heiress of Bergundy. Brothers of Otto were Henry, Margrave of Istria, 1204-09; Berthold V, Patriarch of Aquileia (see n. 11); Egbert, Bishop of Bamberg (see n. 13). Sisters of Otto were Agnes (+1201), wife of King Philip II of France; Gertrude (+1213), wife of King Andrew II of Hungary; St. Hedwig (+1243), wife of Henry, Duke of Silesia-Breslau. Otto took the Cross in 1215 and returned ca. January 1218.

8. Eustorgius of Montagu, Archbishop of Nicosia, 1217-50. He is referred to as a vicar of the Patriarch of Jerusalem in a letter concerning the crusade written to Thibaud, Count of Champagne, and to other French barons. Eustorgius was the brother of Guérin de Montagu, Master of the Hospitallers, and Peter, Master of the Templars.

9. Peter, Bishop of Raab (in Hungary), Suffragan of the primatial see of Strigonium, 1206-18.

10. Thomas, Bishop of Erlau (in Hungary), 1217-24.

11. Berthold V of Meran, Archbishop of Kalocza and Bacs (in Hungary), 1206-18, transferred to Aquileia as Patriarch, 1218-51. He was brother of Duke Otto of Meran (see n. 7) and of Bishop Egbert of Bamberg.

12. Robert of Ableiges, Bishop of Bayeux, 1206-31.

13. Egbert of Meran, Bishop of Bamberg, 1203-37, another brother of Otto of Meran.

14. Engelbert, Bishop of Zeitz (formerly Naumburg), in the Archdiocese of Magdeburg, 1207-42.

15. Otto of Aldenburg, Bishop of Münster, 1204-18.

16. Otto VI, Bishop of Utrecht, 1215-28.

17. Walter of Avesnes (in Flanders) left home in 1217, but had already returned by the spring of 1218. His family contributed several members to the crusades, among whom Jacques of Avesnes had been conspicuous on the Third Crusade.

Chapter 2

The Patriarch of Jerusalem,[1] with great humility on the part of the clergy and the people, reverently lifted up the wood of the life-giving Cross, and set out from Acre on the sixth day after the feast of All Saints [Nov. 6, 1217], into the camp of the Lord which had moved to Recordane.[2] Now this sweet wood had been preserved up to this time, even after the loss of the Holy Land. When the conflict of the Saracens with the Christians was threatening in the time of Saladin, as we have learned from our ancestors, the Cross was cut in pieces; part was carried into battle and was lost there,[3] and part was preserved, which now is displayed. With such a standard, we advanced in orderly array, through the plain of Faba[4] as far as the fountain of Tubania,[5] toiling much on that day; and when we had sent scouts ahead, seeing the dust that was being stirred up by our enemies, we were uncertain whether they were hastening to attack us or to flee. On the following day we set out through the mountains of Gilboa,[6] which were on our right, with a swamp on the left, to Bethsan[7] where the enemy had pitched camp; but fearing the arrival of the army of the living God, that was so numerous, and that was proceeding in so orderly a way, they broke camp and fled, leaving the land to be devastated by the soldiers of Christ. Thence, crossing the Jordan on the vigil of Saint Martin [Nov. 11], we washed our bodies at leisure in it, and we rested throughout two days in the same place, finding an abundance of food and fodder; then on the shore of the Sea of Galilee we made three days' rest, wandering through places in

1. Ralph of Merencourt, former Bishop of Sidon, Patriarch of Jerusalem 1214-25.
2. South of Acre; today known as Chirbet Kurdâne.
3. At the battle of Hattin (July 4, 1187), when Saladin destroyed the army of the kingdom of Jerusalem.
4. Al-Fula, directly southeast of Nazareth.
5. West of Nazareth and known today as Ain Tubaûn.
6. A mountainous region and city, east of the Jordan. The mountain is known today as Jebel Osha.
7. Southwest of the Sea of Tiberias; Bethsan, or Beisan, the ancient Scythopolis.

which Our Savior deigned to work miracles, and conversed with men in His corporal presence. We looked upon Bethsaida,[8] the city of Andrew and Peter, then reduced to a small casale; places were pointed out to us where Christ called His disciples, walked on the sea with dry feet, fed the multitudes in the desert, went up into the mountain alone to pray, and the place where He ate with His disciples after the resurrection; and thus we returned to Acre, carrying our sick and our needy brethren through Capharnaum[9] on beasts of burden.

Chapter 3

In the second raid we approached the foot of Mount Tabor, finding first a lack of water, but afterwards plenty when we dug for it. Our leaders despaired of the ascent of the mountain until, after a Saracen boy had told them that the camp could be seized, they formed a plan. Indeed, on the first Sunday of the Advent of the Lord [Dec. 3], when the gospel was read—"Go into the town that is over against you"[1]—the Patriarch went forward with the sign of the Cross, with bishops and clergy, up the ascent of the mountain, praying and singing psalms. Although the mountain was steep on all sides and high, and apparently impossible to ascend beyond the well-trodden footpath, nevertheless the knights and their attendants, horsemen and foot soldiers, ascended manfully. John, King of Jerusalem, with the army of the Lord, overthrew the chatelain and the emir together in the first attack; he reduced to flight and terror the defenders of the fort, who, to defend the mountain, fearlessly resisted the enemy outside the gates. But the King then lost as much in merit by descending as he had gained by ascending; for in descending on the same Sunday and making others descend, he gave

8. A ruined town on the northeast side of the Lake of Galilee, at the mouth of the Jordan. Probably the present et-Tell.
9. A ruined city on the western shore of the Sea of Galilee, probably the present Tell Hum.

1. Matthew 21:2.

courage to the infidel by the space of time that was granted to them; but we do not know by what judgment of God or by what plan of the leaders the army of the Lord descended then and withdrew ingloriously; this, however, we do know, that the eye of the human mind cannot penetrate the abysses of divine decrees. Now many Templars and Hospitallers and certain seculars were wounded in the second ascent of the mountain when they had received forces from the camp, but few died. We believe that Christ Our Lord reserved this triumph of the mountain for Himself alone, since He ascended it with a few disciples, pointing out there the glory of the future resurrection. Furthermore, in the first and second raids, the Christians carried off with them a very great multitude of captives, men and women, and even children. Now the Bishop of Acre[2] baptized the little ones, whom he could win over by a gift or by a prayer, and apportioning them among religious women, he arranged for them to receive instruction.

Chapter 4

On the third raid,[1] in which the Patriarch, with the sign of the Cross, and the holy pontiffs took no part, we sustained many losses and hardships, as much through highwaymen, as by the severity of the winter, especially on our journey on the vigil of the Nativity of the Lord [Dec. 24], when many poor men and beasts perished from cold, and on the holy night itself, when we endured a severe storm on land, produced

2. Jacques de Vitry, a famous historian of the crusades, Bishop of Acre, Cardinal-Bishop of Tusculum, born ca. 1160, died 1240. He preached a crusade against the Albigensians 1210-13, and was on the expedition against Damietta, 1218-20. Shortly before his death he refused the Patriarchate of Jerusalem. His chief historical work for the crusades is found in his letters to Pope Honorius, and especially in his *Historia Orientalis seu Hierosolymitana*, which gives an eye-witness account of the Holy Land in the 13th century. This includes a geographical description of the country and a description of the magnetic compass. What is called Book III of this work is really part of the present work of Oliver.

1. This expedition went towards Beaufort (Sakif Arnûn), a twin fortress to Toron, and situated at the other side of Nahr Litani.

by wind and rain in the country of Tyre and Sidon near Sarepta.

Chapter 5

After this, the army of the Lord was divided into four parts. The King of Hungary and the King of Cyprus set out for Tripoli, where the youthful King of Cyprus ended his days.[1] After a short delay, the King of Hungary withdrew, to the great detriment of the Holy Land;[2] he took away with him pilgrims also, and helmets, horses, and beasts of burden, with weapons, although he was repeatedly warned by the Patriarch that he should not retreat thus; finally, being excommunicated, he departed stubbornly with his retinue. Another division of lazy and cowardly pilgrims who, lying down, consumed the abundance of temporal things, remained in Acre. But the King of Jerusalem and the Duke of Austria, with the Hospitallers of Saint John[3] and the bishops mentioned above, and certain others, in a short time manfully and faithfully strengthened the fort in Caesarea of Palestine, although the arrival of the enemy was frequently announced. Through this fort, God granting, the city itself will be restored. In the basilica of the Prince of the Apostles, the Patriarch with six bishops solemnly celebrated the feast of the Purification [Feb. 2, 1218]. Moreover the Templars[4] with

1. Hugh I, a Lusignan, died on January 10, 1218, at the age of twenty-three.

2. Andrew had become sick during the early part of the crusade, and had gone to Acre. He was present in Tripoli at the marriage of Bohemond IV with Melisende, sister of Hugh I. Not long afterwards (early in 1218), he returned to Europe by way of Anatolia.

3. The Knights Hospitallers of St. John of Jerusalem, a powerful and wealthy military order. They began in 1092 with the building of a hospital for pilgrims, and followed a rule based on that of St. Augustine. From 1309 to 1523 they were known as the Knights of Rhodes, and from 1530 to 1798 as the Knights of Malta. It is still a religious and secular order in the Catholic church, and there are both Anglican and Lutheran branches, the famous St. John's Ambulance Corps, which did such fine work in England during the recent war, being a subsidiary.

4. The Knights of the Temple, founded in 1118 for the defense of the Christian kingdom of Jerusalem, got their name from their headquarters near the Temple in Jerusalem. They followed a rule especially written for them by St. Bernard. They became the most powerful of the military orders, and were immensely wealthy. To please King Philip the Fair, Pope Clement V suppressed them in 1312.

Lord Walter of Avesnes and some pilgrim helpers, and the Hospitallers from the House of the Teutons,[5] began to refortify the Pilgrims' Castle,[6] which was formerly called Destroit. This is located in the diocese of Caesarea between Caiphas and Caesarea. Its location is as follows:

Chapter 6

A large and lofty promontory overhangs the sea, naturally fortified by cliffs to the north, the west, and the south; toward the east is a strong tower erected some time ago by the Templars, and held as well in war as in time of truce. Now the tower was placed there originally because of bandits who threatened strangers ascending to Jerusalem along the narrow path, and descending from it; it was not far from the sea, and on account of the narrow path it was called Destroit. When the fort of Caesarea was built and completed, the Templars, digging constantly crosswise through the promontory, and laboring for six weeks, finally came upon the first foundation, where the ancient wall appeared thick and long. Money also was found there in a coinage unknown to modern times, which was conferred by the goodness of the Son of God on His soldiers to alleviate their expenses and labors. Next, while they were digging and carrying out sand in an anterior section, another shorter wall was found, and between the flat surface of the walls fountains of fresh water freely gushed forth; the Lord also supplied an abundance of stones and cement. Two towers were built at the front of the

5. The Teutonic Knights were a military order which had its beginning in a tent-hospital for Germans during the siege of Acre in 1189. Its members were German priests, knights, and serving brothers. In the 13th century they conquered and took possession of pagan Prussia, but declined after 1400 from defeats inflicted by the Poles. They turned Lutheran in the 16th century, were secularized in 1805, and were reorganized in Austria in 1834 as a Catholic order to care for the sick. The order now contains professed knights, priests, and sisters. In addition, it exists as a noble order of honor.

6. Athlit, along the coast of Palestine, was fortified at the same time as Caesarea. It is southeast of the edge of Mount Carmel. The Franks had occupied it in the 11th century, and built the tower of Destroit on the last spur of Mount Carmel. Walter of Avesnes called himself its godfather, and referred to the fort as Château-Pélerin.

fort of hewn and fitted stones of such greatness that one stone is with difficulty drawn in a cart by two oxen. Both towers are one hundred feet in length and seventy-four in width. Their thickness encloses two sheds to protect soldiers. Their height rising up much exceeds the height of the promontory. Between the two towers a new and high wall was completed with ramparts; and by a wonderful artifice, armed horsemen can go up and down within. Likewise another wall slightly distant from the towers extends from one side of the sea to the other, having a spring of living water enclosed. The promontory is encircled on both sides by a high new wall, as far as the rocks. The fort contains an oratory with a palace and several houses. The primary advantage of this building is that the assembly of Templars, having been led out of Acre, a sinful city and one filled with all uncleanness, will remain in the garrison of this fort up until the restoration of the walls of Jerusalem. The territory of this fortress abounds in fisheries, salt mines, woods, pastures, fields, and grass; it charms its inhabitants with vines that have been or are to be planted, by gardens and orchards. Between Acre and Jerusalem there is no fortification which the Saracens hold, and therefore the unbelievers are harmed greatly by that new fortress; and with the fear of God pursuing them, they are forced to abandon these cultivated regions. This structure has a naturally good harbor which will be better when aided by artifice; it is six miles away from Mount Tabor. The construction of this castle is presumed to have been the cause of the destruction of the other, because in the long wide plain, which lies between the mountainous districts of this camp and of Mount Tabor, no one could safely plough or sow or reap because of fear of those who lived in it.

Chapter 7

The Bishop of Münster[1] fell asleep in the Lord at Caesarea. Master Thomas,[2] a theologian and a good and clear-minded

1. Bishop Otto died on March 6, 1218, at Caesarea.
2. Nothing further is known of him.

doctor, brought to an end his last day at the Castle of the Son of God.[3]

Chapter 8

After this the army of the Lord returned to Acre. The bishops of Germany and many others prepared themselves to cross the sea after having delayed a short time in the Land of Promise. There was expected a second new passage, and especially a fleet coming from the north,[1] which it was hoped would sail through the narrow sea of Carthage. From the beginning of the preaching of the Cross of Christ, the province of Cologne, with great zeal and also at enormous expense, prepared almost three hundred ships, some of which survived, but others perished from the force of a storm; but a large part arrived at Acre with great courage on the part of the warriors. Discord arose there when certain ones wished to proceed, and others desired to spend the winter in the siege of that most powerful fort which is called Alcatia.[2] And there the fleet was divided: part spent the winter at Gaeta and Corneto; the other part besieged Alcatia under two leaders, Count William of Holland[3] and Count George of Wied.[4] This fort [Alcatia] was captured by the Germans and the Frisians. Until that time they had carried on the siege against a great multitude of Saracens whom the Templars

3. The Castle of the Son of God was the same as the Château-Pélerin.

1. This journey is described in *De Itinere Frisonum* taken from Emo's *Chronicon*, and edited by Röhricht in *Quinti Belli Sacri Scriptores Minores*, pp. 59-70. Three hundred ships were prepared at Cologne. Some remained, others perished, but the majority came to Lisbon in Portugal. The fleet left by the Lauwerzee on May 31, 1216, and arrived at Acre on April 26, 1218.

2. Alcacer de Sol, on the Rio Sado, west of Setubal in Portugal.

3. William I, Count of Holland, 1204-36, of the House of Petersheim, was under excommunication when he took the Cross. He led the Frisians in Spain, and fought very bravely against the Mohammedans. On September 15, 1219, he prepared to depart from the crusade. By April 19, 1220, he was with Frederick II.

4. Count George of Wied was the leader of the Frisian fleet against Spain and Egypt. He was a brother of Dietrich, Archbishop of Trier, 1212-42, and coleader (with Count William of Holland) of the fleet that sailed from the Lauwerzee.

and the Knights of Saint James[5] fought manfully, together with the army of the Queen of Portugal.[6] Finally the Saracens were conquered by divine strength; one of their kings was killed, and with him a great many were massacred or led into captivity.[7]

Chapter 9

The province of Cologne was stirred up to the service of the Savior of the world through signs which appeared in heaven. For in the province of Cologne and in the diocese of Münster in a village of Fresia, namely, Bedum, in the month of May on the sixth day before Pentecost [May 16], when the Cross was preached there, a triple form appeared in the heavens, one white toward the north, another toward the south of the same color and shape, a third in the middle, tinted with color, having the fork of a cross, and the figure of a man suspended upon it, with arms raised and extended, with the mark of nails in hands and feet, and with bowed head. This middle one was between two others on which there was no likeness of a human body. At another time and in another place, in a village of Fresia, at the time of the preaching of the Cross, there appeared alongside of the sun a cross of a blue color; more saw this than saw the former. The third apparition was in the diocese of Utrecht in the village of Dokkum where Saint Boniface was martyred. When on the feast of the same martyr [June 5] many thousands had assembled there for the station of the same martyr, there appeared a large white cross as if one beam had been artificially placed over another.

5. Oliver uses the term "Spatarians" for the Knights of the Military Order of St. James of the Sword (de la Spatha), founded in Spain about the year 1158. Their chief purpose was to aid Christianity by war upon the Saracens. Their distinguishing badge was a red sword on a white cloak.

6. The King of Portugal, 1211-23, was Alfonso II. His wife, whom he married in 1207 or 1208, was Urraca, daughter of Alfonso III, King of Castile.

7. The *Gesta Crucigerorum Rhenanorum* (*Quinti Belli, Sacri Scriptores Minores*, ed. Röhricht, pp. 27-56) and the *De Itinere Frisonum* (*ibid.*, pp. 57-70) give few details about this capture of Alcacer (known to the Arabs as Kafr Abû Danes under the rule of Abd Allah ibn Muhammed ibn Wazir).

This sign we all saw. Now it moved gradually from the north to the south. But we believe that the two apparitions were manifested so that all the ambiguity of the first vision might be removed, as the Apostle says about the resurrection of Christ, "that He appeared to Cephas, afterwards to the eleven apostles, and next to more than five hundred brethren."[1]

Chapter 10

In the year of grace 1218, in the month of March, ships[1] began to sail to the port of Acre from the province of Cologne with other small ships from the province of Bremen and Trier. Thus was accomplished that plan formed in the Lateran Council at Rome under the Lord Pope Innocent of good memory, for leading the army of the Christians into the land of Egypt. Therefore in the month of May, after the Ascension of the Lord [May 24], when the ships had been prepared, and the galleys had been equipped with arms, and the other ships had been loaded, there set out from Acre, John, King of Jerusalem; the Patriarch with the bishops of Nicosia, Bethlehem,[2] and Acre; the Duke of Austria with the three Houses,[3] and a copious multitude of Christians. The fleet was ordered to assemble at the Castle of the Son of God, which is called the Castle of the Pilgrims; then with a north wind blowing, when the King, the Duke, and the masters of the Houses came to the appointed place, the host of the Lord set out under full sail, arriving at the harbor of Damietta on the third day. Now the above-mentioned leaders, since they had made a slight delay at the castle, could not follow after the host until the sixth day after their departure from the harbor of Acre. Many also who had not been prepared and who

1. I Corinthians 15:5-6.

1. The Latin word *cogones* has here been freely translated "ships."
2. The Patriarch Ralph, the bishops of Nicosia and Acre, and the Duke of Austria have been identified above. The Bishop of Bethlehem was Regnier, *ca.* 1207-27.
3. The Templars, Hospitallers, and Teutonic Knights.

made some delay at Acre, after those who sailed first, either remained there entirely or were driven back into Acre by the violence of the winds; or, being tossed about for three or four weeks, were delayed on the sea. The Archbishop of Rheims[4] and the Bishop of Limoges[5] remained in Acre because of their advanced years. The Bishop of Limoges died there; the Archbishop of Rheims, having returned on the passage of the Holy Cross, perished on the way.

Now upon coming to land at the port of Damietta, they chose the Count of Saarbrücken[6] as their leader, and captured the hostile land on the third day [May 29] without any loss of blood, before the King and the aforesaid dukes followed them. For when a few Saracens advanced upon the knights at the harbor, a certain Frisian, with his right knee planted on the ground, turned his shield with his left hand, and brandished and hurled an iron spear with the right. A Saracen horseman watched him, thinking he was playing, when suddenly horse and rider, struck down by the Frisian, perished and fell to the ground. When the others fled, abandoning their baggage, the Christians fixed the boundaries of the camp between the seashore and the bank of the river Nile, to the great admiration of those following when they saw the tents that had been set up. God brought about this wonderful fact, that upon their first arrival the water of the river, though it was joined to the sea and on many occasions afterwards was of a salty taste, was drawn up fresh all the way to the casale which is almost a mile above Damietta. A short time after the arrival of the Christians there took place an almost complete eclipse of the moon; and although it usually comes from natural causes at the time of full moon, yet because Our Savior says, "There shall be signs in the sun and moon,"[7] we interpreted this eclipse to the disfavor of the Saracens, as if it portended the failure of the very ones who

4. Alberic, Archbishop of Rheims since 1207, who died on December 24, 1218.

5. John de Veirac, Bishop of Limoges, 1197(98)-1218.

6. Simon II, Count of Saarbrücken, 1211-33.

7. Luke 21:25.

impute the moon to themselves, putting great strength in the waning or waxing moon. Now it is read in Quintus Curtius[8] that when Alexander the Macedonian, the hammer of the whole world, set out against Darius and Porus from Greece into Asia, and his well-ordered battle lines proceeded on this side and that, there occurred an eclipse of the moon. Alexander, interpreting this in favor of the Greeks against the Medes and the Persians, encouraged his men, fought against Darius, and conquered him.

Chapter 11

A tower located in the middle of the river had to be captured before crossing. The Frisians, however, who were impatient of delay, crossed the Nile and carried off the animals of the Saracens. Wishing to pitch camp on the farther shore, they held their ground, fighting against the Saracens who came out of their city to oppose them. They were recalled through obedience because it did not seem wise to our leaders that a tower filled with pagans should be left behind the Christians. Meanwhile the Duke of Austria and the Hospitallers of Saint John prepared two ladders on two ships, and the Teutons and Frisians fortified a third ship with bulwarks, setting up a small fortress on the top of the mast without hanging a ladder. Their head, their leader, and their counselor was Count Adolph of Berg,[1] a noble and powerful man, the brother of the Archbishop of Cologne.[2] The Count died at Damietta before the tower was captured. The ladders of the Duke and of the Hospitallers were directed against the tower about the time of the feast of Saint John the Baptist [June 24], with the Saracens defending it manfully. The ladder of the Hospitallers was shattered and crashed with the mast, hurl-

8. *Historiae Alexandri Magni*, IV, 40. This is the only reference made to the name of a classical writer throughout the present work.

1. Count Adolph V, 1189-1218. He died before Damietta on August 7, 1218.
2. St. Engelbert II, just made archbishop earlier in the year 1218. He died in 1225.

ing its warriors headlong; the ladder of the Duke, being broken in like manner at almost the same time, sent up to heaven soldiers who were vigorous and well armed, wounded in body to the advantage of their souls, crowned with a glorious martyrdom. The overjoyed Egyptians, mocking us violently, raised their voices, beating drums and sounding sackbuts;[3] gloom and sadness invaded the Christians. But the ship of the Germans and Frisians cast anchor between the tower and the city, causing great losses to the Egyptians through its ballistae,[4] which had been set up within, especially to those who were standing on the bridge that extended between the city and the tower. The ship itself, however, was being quite violently attacked by the warriors of the city, by the javelins of the tower and of the bridge, and by Greek fire. Finally it was seized upon by the fire; and although the Christians feared that it would be entirely destroyed, its defenders bravely extinguished the flames. Likewise pierced by arrows within and without, both in that fortress placed on the top of the mast and even on the ropes of the rigging, the ship, bearing the great honor of Christianity, was brought back to its position. No slight damage was dealt out and endured by one ship of the Templars, fortified by bulwarks which were held alongside of the tower at the time of this assault.

Chapter 12

However, we realized that the tower could neither be captured by the blows of petraries[1] or of trebuchets[2] (for this was attempted for many days); nor by bringing the fort closer, because of the depth of the river; nor by starvation, because of the surroundings of the city; nor by undermining, because of the roughness of the water flowing about. With the Lord

3. An obsolete musical instrument, a bass trumpet with a slide like that of a trombone for altering the pitch.
4. An ancient military engine resembling a bow, stretched with cords and thongs, used to hurl stones or other missiles.

1. A military engine of the medieval period for hurling stones.
2. This also was a medieval military engine for casting heavy missiles.

showing us how and providing an architect,[3] and with the Germans and the Frisians providing supplies and labor, we joined two ships which we bound together sturdily by means of beams and ropes and so prevented (by their closely connected structure) the danger of drifting. We erected four masts and the same number of sailyards, setting up on the summit a strong fortress joined with poles and a network fortification. We covered it with skins about its circumference, as a protection from the attacks of their machine, and over its top as a defense against the Greek fire. Under the fortress was made a ladder, hung by very strong ropes and stretching out thirty cubits beyond the prow. This task having been successfully completed in a short time, the leaders of the army were invited to see it, so that if anything was lacking that ought to be supplied by material or by human ingenuity, they would point it out. They replied that such a work of wood had never before been wrought upon the sea. We realized that we must hasten, because, by frequent blows of the machines, the bridge which conveyed the enemies of the faith from the city to the tower in great part had been destroyed. Therefore on the sixth day before the feast of Saint Bartholomew [Aug. 18], we made a procession barefoot to the Holy Cross with devotion on the part of our people. After humbly imploring divine assistance that the affair might be free from all envy and empty boasting, we summoned to the execution of this task some men of every nation that was then in the army, although the nation of Germans and Frisians would suffice to fill and direct the ships.

Chapter 13

On the feast of Saint Bartholomew [Aug. 24], the sixth day, since the Nile had violently overflowed and the force of the waters greatly hindered our work, with the greatest difficulty and danger this engine was dragged against the torrent from the place in which it had been made, to the tower. A smaller ship, a companion of this machine, went along spreading its

3. Oliver himself.

sails. The clergy, barefoot, walked as suppliants on the shore. When they had come to the tower, that twofold arrangement could not be turned around toward the west side, but by moving up it was placed directly toward the northern section. The ropes and anchors were finally made firm, although the force of the flooding waters strove to drive it back. Six or more machines were drawn up on the top of the towers of the city, and were placed there to shatter it. Now one, more dangerous than the others, being destroyed after a few blows, ceased its action; but the others without any intermission cast out stones like hail. And no less a danger did the first ship withstand, located at the foot of the tower. The Greek fire from the tower of the river close at hand came from the city afar like lightning and was able to inspire fear; but by sour liquid and gravel, and other means of extinguishing it, those who were toiling were aided.

The Patriarch lay prostrate in the dust before the wood of the Cross; the clergy, standing barefoot, garbed in liturgical robes, cried out to heaven. The defenders of the tower with lances extended, smeared the front of the ladder with oil; next they added fire which caused it to burst into flames. And when the Christians who were on it ran to put out the fire, they pressed on the head of the ladder with their weight so much that the movable bridge placed near its edge was made to bend. The standard bearer of the Duke of Austria fell from the ladder, and the Saracens captured the banner of the Duke. The Babylonians,[1] thinking that they were victorious, shouted madly, disturbing the air with their clamor. The Christians, descending from their horses, threw themselves down in supplication, beating their hands; their faces streamed with tears of sorrow as they protested the pity they had for those who were enduring peril in the depth of the river, and the loss of all Christendom. In answer to this devotion of the people and the raising of their hands to heaven, divine kindness lifted the ladder, the tears of the faithful extinguished the fire; and thus our men, with renewed vigor, manfully fought with the defenders of the tower by means

1. The Mohammedans of Egypt were often referred to as Babylonians, because Cairo was usually referred to as Babylon, owing to its closeness to the ancient city of that name in Egypt.

of swords, pikes, clubs, and other weapons. A certain young knight of the diocese of Liège was the first to ascend the tower; a certain young Frisian, holding a flail by which grain is usually threshed, but which was prepared for fighting by an interweaving with chains, lashed out bravely to the right and to the left, knocked down a certain man holding the saffron standard of the Sultan and took the banner away from him. One came after another, vanquishing the enemy, who were known to be hard and cruel in their resistance. O ineffable kindness of God! O unexplainable joy of Christians! After lamentation and grief, after weeping and groaning, we saw joy and triumph. "We praise Thee, O God,"[2] "Blessed be the Lord God of Israel,"[3] and other canticles of thanksgiving to the heavens we sang for joy, our voices being mingled with tears and our praises repeated.

Chapter 14

Meanwhile the Saracens, who had withdrawn to the inner part of the tower, having put fire under the top part of the tower, burned it; our men, though victorious, retreated over the ladder, not being able to stand the heat. But the bridge, which had been prepared in the lower part of the fortification, was let down to the narrow foot of the tower, with deep waters surging about on all sides. With iron hammers the victors attacked the door while the Saracens who were within defended it. Both fortifications remained impregnable; the rungs of the ladder, in part, and the circuit of the work which was held together by very strong ropes were pierced by blows of the machines. From the ninth hour of the sixth day until the tenth hour of the following Saturday [Aug. 25] this danger lasted. But the net-like arrangement which protected the ladder remained unharmed, along with the fort in which were stationed the ballistae and the petraries, which protected them. Finally, being enclosed in the tower, the Saracens sought a conference, and, under a guarantee

2. A hymn sung in the office of Matins after the 9th lesson, and as a prayer of thanksgiving at times of great rejoicing. It is called the Ambrosian Hymn, but the author is unknown.
3. The canticle of Zachary (Luke 1: 68-79), said daily at Lauds.

that their lives would be spared, they surrendered to the Duke of Austria, except those who on the preceding night had thrown themselves headlong through the windows and escaped the narrow bounds of the tower; several of them were drowned in the river and perished. But the captives numbered one hundred men.

Chapter 15

Although from that day the Babylonians were confused and terrified, and, as it was thought, prepared for flight, our leaders fell into idleness and laziness according to their custom. They invented a motive for deferring negotiations, and they did not imitate Judas Macchabeus who "seeing that the time served him"[1] gave no rest to the enemy.

Chapter 16

The ships prepared to withdraw. A great multitude of Frisians and Teutons set out in the next passage of the Holy Cross. In that passage[1] came certain Romans, and after that the Bishop of Albano, the Delegate of the Apostolic See,[2] and with him a Roman prince;[3] next the Archbishop of Bordeaux[4] who made a useful delay; the bishops of Angers,[5] Mantua,[6]

1. Macchabees 12:1.

1. August and September 1218.
2. Pelagius Galvani, a Spaniard or Portuguese by birth. Cardinal-Bishop of Albano, 1211-40. He has been blamed by many for the ultimate failure of the crusade. His unwillingness to accept terms considered favorable by the Christian lay leaders was due to his anxiety to capture Cairo itself. His high-handed methods alienated many of the lay lords. In the Church he had a distinguished career. Pope Innocent III made him Cardinal-Deacon of the Title of S. Lucia, then Cardinal-Priest in 1206. He was Papal Legate on the crusade, as Oliver mentions. After its disastrous ending he returned to Europe and was employed by Pope Honorius III on many occasions. He died in Monte Cassino, January 27, 1240.
3. This was James, Count of Andria. Perhaps he was a relative of Hugh I, Duke of Andria, ca. 1173-1240.
4. William II, Amanieu de Geniès, 1207-27.
5. William of Beaumont, Bishop of Angers, 1202-40. He became Archbishop in 1207.
6. Henry, Bishop of Mantua, 1193-1220(25?).

Humana,[7] and Salpi;[8] next Master Robert of Courçon, Cardinal-Bishop of the title of Saint Stephen on Monte Celio;[9] the bishops of Paris,[10] Gerona,[11] Erlau,[12] and Hungary, who died before the crossing of the river on the sand of Damietta, and Cardinal Robert likewise. The Count of Nevers [13] came also, who, when danger threatened, retreated, to the scandal of the Christians. The Count of La Marche,[14] and the Count of Bar[15] and his son,[16] Brother William of Chartres, Master of the army of the Temple,[17] Hervé of Vierzon,[18] Ithier of Toucy,[19] Oliver, son of the King of England,[20] and many others of the knightly order, and common people, ended their days at Damietta. Many martyrs for Christ, more confessors of Christ, being delivered from human cares at Damietta, went to the Lord.

Chapter 17

"He is wise in heart and mighty in strength Who doth great things and unsearchable things without number and marvelous. Who judges those that are high, Who places the humble

7. Gerard III, first mentioned in 1204, and who was dead by 1228.

8. Unknown.

9. Chancellor of the University of Paris, and Cardinal, 1212-19. He was a brother of Walter of Nemours, Chamberlain of France. The two brothers departed for the crusade in 1218.

10. Peter of Nemours, Archbishop of Paris, 1208-19.

11. Raymond of Palafolls, Archbishop of Gerona, 1214-18.

12. Thomas of Hungary did not die as is stated here, but returned home in September 1218.

13. See note 18, below.

14. Hugh II of Angoulême of La Marche, 1208-49.

15. Milo III, Count of Bar-sur-Seine since 1189. He died on August 18, 1219 at the siege of Damietta. His two sons also were killed there.

16. Walter of Puiset, son of Milo.

17. William of Puiset, called William of Chartres, son of Milo and brother of Walter, Master of the Temple, 1209-19.

18. Hervé IV of Donzy, Count of Nevers since 1199, by his marriage to Mahaut, daughter of Peter of Courtenay and his wife Agnes. He died on January 22, 1223.

19. Perhaps a descendant of Ithier III, oldest son of Narjot I, Lord of Toucy, 1147-73. Ithier III had gone on the crusade with Louis VII.

20. Oliver was an illegitimate son of John Lackland, King of England, 1199-1216.

on high."[1] He alone was magnified in the siege of Damietta. For not as in other expeditions against the Saracens, when various opportunities were arranged through human wisdom or the agency of the warriors, but through Himself did He work miraculously through the power of His divinity what man did not presume to seek; giving honor not to kings or other princes or nations, but to His Name, that the prophetic promise might be fulfilled in us sinners: "The Lord will fight for you and you will hold your peace."[2]

Chapter 18

After the tower had been captured that was located in the depths of the river Nile, Saphadin,[1] grown old with evil days and sickness, the disinheritor of his cousins and the usurper of the kingdoms of Asia, died and was buried in hell. Afterwards on the feast of Saint Denis [Oct. 9] the Saracens, coming unexpectedly with armed galleys and invading the most important of the camps where the Romans had set up tents, were repulsed by a small band of Christians; King John of Jerusalem fought manfully there at the exhortation of the Bishop of Bethlehem, when he pursued them as they ran back quickly to their galleys; nevertheless, they were unable to escape the swords of their pursuers and the whirling of the river. Now, like the Egyptians formerly in the raging waters of the Red Sea, so in the Nile about one thousand were drowned, as we learned afterwards from the Saracens.

On the feast of Saint Demetrius [Oct. 26], who is said to have been the uterine brother of the blessed Denis, the enemy at dawn invaded the camp of the Templars, and

---

1. Job 9:4; 5:9; 5:11.
2. Exodus 14:14.

---

1. Malik-al-Adil Seif ed Din, brother of Saladin, died on August 31, 1218. Of his many sons, two deserve mention here: Malik-al-Kamil Mohammed, Sultan of Egypt; and Malik-al-Moadden Isa, known to the Christians as Coradin, Lord of Damascus. At one time Richard the Lion-Hearted had proposed that Saphadin marry his sister, the widowed Queen of Sicily. Saphadin had united the empire of Saladin at the expense of Saladin's own sons, whom he dispossessed of their heritage.

though causing us a slight loss, they were driven away by our alert horsemen, to the bridge which they had built a short distance from us in the upper part of the river; they were killed to the number of five hundred, as we learned from deserters.

Chapter 19

Next, since many of the Christian people were pleasing to the Lord, it was necessary that temptation should prove them. Jonas, being cast out into the sea because of the trouble of the tempest, and being shut up in the belly of a fish, returned to dry land when he had been proved. The Apostle escaped when he had been tried by a threefold shipwreck; the people of the Lord deserved to be tried when they had practised a three days' fast, which the clergy observed obediently on bread and water, and when many processions had been ordered by the venerable Lord Pelagius, the Bishop of Albano, Legate of the Apostolic See. For on the vigil of Saint Andrew the Apostle [Nov. 29], in the middle of the night, the waves of the sea rose, swelling and making a terrible advance even to the camp of the faithful; the river, rushing in from the other direction, took us unaware. The tents floated off, the food supply was destroyed, fishes of the river and of the sea, as though fearing nothing, piled into our sleeping quarters, and we caught them with our hands, delights nevertheless which we were willing to be without. And unless, by the plan of the Holy Ghost, preparations had been made beforehand[1] on the rampart which had been made for other uses, the sea joined with the river would have dragged off to the enemy the men with the animals, and the ships with the weapons and food supplies. This danger, however, four ships, upon which had been erected fortresses to capture the city, did not escape; in one attack, they, along with a fifth ship which was caught in their midst, were driven to the opposite shore by the force of the winds, and were burned before our eyes with Greek fire. The Lord spared the labors of the Fri-

1. In the middle of October or early November.

sians and the Germans by whom the tower had been captured. Laden ships which were standing in the port of the sea were lost when their ropes were suddenly broken. This storm lasted for three continuous days. When this had elapsed, the Lord "Who consoles His people in every tribulation, comforts in all our afflictions, commanded the wind and the sea to be still, making it cease from raging."[2]

Chapter 20

Besides, many of the army were struck down by a certain plague against which physicians could find no remedy in all their skill.[1] A sudden pain attacked the feet and legs, and at the same time corrupt flesh covered the gums and teeth, taking away the power of chewing; a horrible blackness darkened the shins, and so having been afflicted with a long stretch of illness, very many went to the Lord with much suffering. Certain ones, surviving until spring, escaped, being delivered by the advantage of heat.

Chapter 21

After the aforesaid tempest, the ships were prepared to cross the river; these, going up at great risk between the city and the captured tower, were greatly retarded by Greek fire and javelins. Wherefore it happened that one ship of the Templars,[1] carried away by the violence of the current, was cast over near the side of the city toward the enemy, who for a

2. See Matthew 8:26; II Corinthians 1:4; Jonas 1:15.

1. This disease reminds us of the troubles suffered by Richard on his crusade. He had pains in the mouth and lips, apparently from Vincent's infection or trench mouth. See Ambroise, The Crusade of Richard the Lion Heart, tr. and ed. by M. J. Hubert and J. L. LaMonte (New York, 1941), ll. 405-08, p. 196. The sickness described by Oliver seems to have been even more acute and resembles the disease known in modern times as scurvy.

1. This is a chronological error. The loss of this ship occurred in early November before the storm.

long time assailed it with barbots[2] and grappling irons, hurling out Greek fire and stones from the towers above; and
since they could not prevail on account of the bravery of the
defenders, they eagerly climbed up the ship, and throwing
themselves headlong into it, descended upon the Templars.
When they had fought there for a long time, the ship at last
was pierced (whether by the enemy or by our own men we
do not know) and sought the depths, drowning Egyptians
with Christians, so that the top of the mast scarcely appeared
above the water. And as Samson "killed many more at his
death than he had killed before in his life,"[3] so also those
martyrs dragged into the abyss of the waters along with
themselves more than they could have killed with swords.
But the citizens of Damietta mourned their bloody victory
for almost seven days. Thereupon, while repairing the bridge
they left a narrow opening, so that our ships could not go
up without danger. But the Germans and the Frisians, fired
with the zeal of righteous indignation, having no help except from heaven, manfully attacked the bridge with the
smaller ship by whose aid the tower had been captured,
and which the Gauls called "Holy Mother." Less than ten
men of the above-mentioned nation climbed the bridge
in the face of all the hardihood of the Babylonians, with
a great multitude of Christians looking on and highly
praising this boldness. They broke it down; and thus, with the
four ships upon which the bridge had been founded, they
returned in triumph, leaving a way free and open for the
ships sailing upward.

Chapter 22

When all this had been so accomplished, the Saracens, while
awaiting the danger which threatened them, fortified the
bank opposite us by means of ramparts and a clay-like substance with high wooden defenses, setting up machines and

2. A small vessel having its deck protected by an arched covering of
leather.
3. Judges 16:30.

petraries there, taking from us the hope of crossing through that place. But from the casale, which is almost a mile away from the city, where this new fortification ended, all across the river they sank ships and fixed stakes in the eddies. Nevertheless the Legate of the Apostolic See, having the good desire of besieging the city, urged the ships gathered higher up to cross. Wherefore the ships, fortified by defenses and fortresses, and also by armed men with galleys and other ships, Christ being their leader, escaped the sunken ships mentioned above. But the enemy, pretending fear, placed three ranks of armed men opposite the position of our ships: one of foot soldiers above the bank with shields, which they call targes, ranged in lines; the second behind them like the first; the third of horsemen, long and terrible, violently harassing the position of the Christians with showers of stones and weapons.

In addition, on the night of the solemnity of Saint Agatha, virgin and martyr [Feb. 5, 1219], when the people of the faithful assembled who were to cross on the following day, rains and winds added much peril and difficulty to our men. But "God is faithful" and "will not permit you to be tempted beyond your strength,"[1] and looking at the camp of His servants, He turned into ease and joy a thing which according to less important causes would have been difficult or impossible, renewing the wonders of His power. After the middle of the night He struck such terror to the Sultan of Babylon and his satraps that, abandoning the camp unknown even to the Egyptians whom he had ranged for resisting, they placed their hope in flight alone. A certain apostate who, having transgresed the law of the Christians for some time, had fought on the side of the Sultan, stood on the bank and cried out in French, "Why do you delay? Why are you afraid? Why do you hesitate? The Sultan has gone away." And having said this he asked to be taken back into a ship so that being put in their power he might give proof to his words. Therefore at early dawn, when the office of the Mass

1. I Corinthians 10:13.

of the feast-day had been begun throughout the oratories of the Christians, these words, "Let us all rejoice in the Lord,"[2] were announced to the Legate, the King, and the others. And so as the Egyptians fled, our men crossed eagerly and quickly with no hindrance from the enemy and no shedding of blood.

But the land of the enemy was so muddy and so difficult to land upon because of the rather deep waters that the horses, being driven without saddles or riders, could scarcely get up. The Templars, leaders in the ascent of the horses, having put up their banners, hurried to the city in a swift march, throwing down the wicked ones who came boldly from the gates to resist those who were advancing. "The axe shall not boast itself against him that cutteth with it nor shall the saw exalt itself against him by whom it is drawn."[3] To what shall we equal or compare this miracle except to that which is read concerning Benadab, King of Syria,[4] who besieged Samaria, reducing it greatly, to whom the Lord sent such terror that he fled abandoning his camp? And as the flight of the Syrians was announced to the Samaritans by the lepers who were at the entrance of the gate, so the flight of the Egyptians was announced by one who was a leper in his soul, that is to say, the aforesaid apostate; and as the people of the Samaritans gathered up the spoils left in the camp of the Syrians, so our army plundered the tents and booty of those who were fleeing; the victors seized many targes and all the galleys, along with the barbots and other ships, which were found below the casale as far as the city, with other spoils. Many warriors, having left their wives and children, fled from Damietta, terrified because of the unexpected crossing. And the city was besieged firmly in a circle, the army being joined together through the arrangement of a bridge touching both banks.

2. These words begin the Introit on the Feast of St. Agatha and on many feasts of the Blessed Virgin.

3. Isaias 10:15.

4. See IV Kings 6:24; 7:3. The last reference applies to the following sentence.

Chapter 23

However, through the idleness and laziness of those whose names God knows, it happened that as Coradin[1] arrived with the men of Aleppo and a great multitude, the enemy with renewed vigor and spirit seized that place [Mar. 3] from which our men had made a miraculous crossing; and thus, as we were besieging the city, they besieged us more dangerously; and unless by divine counsel the first camp which was between the sea and the river had been held by the Germans and Frisians especially, the port would have been taken from us and the whole business, greatly imperiled, would have wavered. But in order that the miracle of the crossing might become more famous, and be unhesitatingly ascribed to Christ alone, the Saracens reached such a point of temerity that at daybreak of the Saturday before "Oculi mei semper" Sunday [Mar. 9],[2] since we did not foresee such a danger, they drew nearer with a great multitude and pressed on as far as the rampart; but by divine assistance they were driven back, with a loss of horsemen and foot soldiers.

Chapter 24

In the year of grace 1219, Jerusalem, the queen of cities, which seemed impregnably fortified, was destroyed within and without by Coradin, son of Saphadin [Mar. 19 or 25].[1] Its walls and towers were reduced to heaps of stones except for the temple of the Lord and the tower of David. The Saracens

---

1. Al-Malik al Moadden Isa of Damascus, 1218-27. He assisted his father and brother in their wars with the Christians, both by bringing aid from Syria to Egypt, and by keeping up diversionary attacks on Christian positions in Syria.
2. The third Sunday of Lent. The Introit of the Mass for this day begins with the words "Oculi mei."

---

1. Jerusalem had been in the hands of the Mohammedans since 1187, when it was surrendered to Saladin. After Coradin destroyed the walls in 1219, he destroyed two fortresses also, Toron and Safita. He did this because he thought that the Christians would retake the city.

took counsel about destroying the glorious sepulchre, and they threatened this through letters which they sent across to the citizens of Damietta for their own consolation; but no one presumed to set his hand to this act of boldness because of reverence for the place. For as they had written in the Koran, the book of their law, they believe that Jesus Christ Our Lord was conceived and born of the Virgin Mary and they protest that He lived without sin as a prophet and more than a prophet; they firmly assert that He gave sight to the blind, cleansed lepers, and raised the dead; they do not deny the word and the spirit of God, and that He ascended alive into heaven. But they do deny His Passion and Death, and also that the divine nature is united to the human nature in Christ. They likewise deny the Trinity of Persons. Therefore they ought to be called heretics rather than Saracens, but the use of the false name prevails. Therefore, at the time of truce, when their wise men went up to Jerusalem, they asked that copies of the Gospels be shown to them. These they kissed and venerated because of the purity of the law which Christ taught, and especially because of the Gospel of Luke: "The Angel Gabriel was sent,"[2] which the learned among them often repeat and recall to mind. But their law, which Mohammed, under the dictation of the devil, gave to the Saracens, and which was written in Arabic by the ministry of Sergius, a monk, an apostate, and a heretic, began from the sword, is upheld by the sword, and will be ended in the sword. Mohammed was unlearned, as he himself gives evidence in his Koran, and what the forenamed heretic dictated, he promulgated and ordered to be observed through threats. For he was dissolute and warlike, and therefore he laid down a law concerning uncleanness and vanity, which those who live carnally on the side of pleasure carefully observe. And as truth and purity fortify our law, so worldly and human fear and carnal pleasure guard their error most firmly.[3]

2. Luke 1:26.
3. Compare the picture given here by Oliver with R. S. Darbishere, "The Moslem Antagonist," *Moslem World*, XXVIII (1938), 258-71.

Chapter 25

On Palm Sunday of the forementioned year [Mar. 31], our enemies, having made many threats that they would destroy themselves or all of us in one day, collected a fearful and innumerable army of horsemen and foot soldiers and rushed upon us, invading our ramparts on all sides, especially the bridge of the Templars and the Duke of Austria, which he was eager to defend with the Germans. The enemy, with picked soldiers, leaped from their horses and fought savagely with the Christians. On this side and that many fell dead and wounded, and finally, climbing the bridge, they burned part of it. The Duke of Austria ordered his men that when the bridge had been abandoned they should give approach and entrance to those who were pressing on us; but they did not presume to enter because of our army, which had ranged its lines as an aid to those defending the fortifications. The women fearlessly brought water and stones, wine and bread to the warriors; the priests persisted in prayer, binding up and blessing the wounds of the injured. On that day, we were not given the opportunity of carrying palms other than crossbows, bows, and arrows, lances and swords and shields, so violently did they attack and harass us from sunrise to almost the tenth hour—they who had come to destroy us in the desire of freeing the city; at last they retreated wearily with great losses.

Chapter 26

The spring passage was not imminent. The Duke of Austria was going to withdraw, he who for a year and a half had fought faithfully for Christ, full of devotion, humility, obedience, and generosity. Besides all the other innumerable expenses which he had incurred in the dealings of war and in private alms, he is believed to have bestowed on the house of the Teutons six thousand marks of silver or more, to obtain land; and on the new fort of the Templars fifty marks of gold.

To it also the Earl of Chester[1] gave fifty marks of silver for the strengthening of its walls and towers.

Chapter 27

On the first of May a great multitude of pilgrims began to withdraw, leaving us in the greatest danger. But our kind and merciful Father, our leader and comrade in arms, Jesus Christ, "the protector and defender of those who hope in Him, for Whom it is easy to save either by many or by few,"[1] did not permit the unbelievers to rush in upon us until new and recent pilgrims arrived with abundant aid; a supply of provisions and horses sent over by divine power gladdened the assembly of the faithful. Therefore, on the feast of the Ascension of the Lord [May 16], when the number of the soldiers of Christ was renewed, the untrustworthy enemy, according to their custom, rushed upon us by land and by water. As they could not prevail, though they made many attempts, they challenged our men particularly near the camp, losing and inflicting losses. But on July 31 they brought forward all the power which they could muster, and after many assaults, finally crossed the ramparts against the army of the Temple. Violently bursting the barriers, they put our foot soldiers to flight, to such an extent that the whole army of the Christians was then endangered. The knights and soldiery of France tried three times to drive them farther back beyond the rampart, but were unable to do so. The Saracens, when our wooden fortifications had been shattered, ranged lines of horsemen and foot soldiers within our walls; their shouts arose as they mocked us; the whole multitude prepared its retinue. Fear welled up in the Christians, but the spirit which came upon Gideon animated the Templars. The

1. Ranulf, Earl of Chester, had helped John Lackland in the civil war in England. On Ash Wednesday, 1215, he took the Cross, and in 1218 set out for the East. He landed soon after the capture of the chain tower. He returned to England about August 1, 1220.

1. Psalms 17:13; I Kings 14:6.

Master of the Temple, with the Marshal and other brothers who were then present, made an attack through a narrow approach and manfully put the unbelievers to flight. The House of the Teutons and the counts and other knights of different nations, seeing the army of the Temple placed in such danger, quickly brought aid through entrances opposite them; thus the foot soldiers of the Saracens threw away their shields and were killed, except those whose headlong flight had snatched them from their killers. Our foot soldiers went out after our horsemen. The enemy retreated a short distance, their armed ranks holding out here and there, until evening twilight put an end to the battle. The Saracens went away first. Bodies of massacred wretches lay strewn near our rampart in great numbers, except those who were wounded seriously or slightly, and were brought back to the camp. Thus on that day did God save those who hoped in Him through the courage of the Templars and of those who, having worked together with them, committed themselves to the conflict. A few of our men were killed or captured.

Chapter 28

Almost all the machines prepared against the city were burned in a many-sided sortie of the defenders of Damietta. The Pisans, the Genoese, and the Venetians[1] stoutly affirmed that they would attack the city by means of four ships upon which ladders hung; "but they were not of the race of those men by whom salvation was brought to Israel;"[2] for they wished to make a name for themselves, going forward with trumpets and reed pipes and many standards. The Legate of the Apostolic See supplied copious funds to them from the common store, the King and others produced ropes and anchors in abundance according as they needed them. And so,

1. These inhabitants of northern Italian cities frequently sent along contingents with the crusaders in return for commercial advantages. Thus, they sided with Pelagius in insisting upon the capture of Damietta, a town that seemed promising for commerce.
2. I Macchabees 5:62.

attacking the city, they killed and wounded many on the first day; and the more often they made an attack afterward, so much the more were the walls strengthened by wooden towers and palisades; the defenders resisted the oncomers even more vigorously and efficaciously, and thus the ladders, injured by fire and several times repaired, were forced to the bank, and the attempt was fruitless. And so it was truly understood that by divine power alone would Damietta be delivered into the hands of the Christians.

Chapter 29

But we, insensible and unmindful of the benefits and wonderful deeds of God, which He had done, "provoked the eyes of His divine majesty"[1] against us through the idleness of the leaders and the complaints of the followers. The foot soldiers reproached the cowardice of the horsemen, the horsemen made light of the risks of the foot soldiers when they went out against the Saracens. Therefore it happened that on the feast of the beheading of Saint John the Baptist [Aug. 29], with our common faults urging us on, although scarcely any were to be found who would remain in the custody of the camp, we led forth a naval and land army and proceeded to the camp of the Babylonians between the sea and the river, where fresh water could not be found to drink. But taking up their tents, they pretended flight; and when our men had advanced to a point where it was clear that our adversaries did not wish to meet us in open combat, our leaders began a long debate whether they should advance or retreat; the feeling among them was divided. Meanwhile the ranks were scattered except for a group of those whom obedience bound in military discipline. The knights of Cyprus,[2] who were on the right flanks, showed their timidity to the Saracens as they

1. Isaias 3:8.
2. The knights of Cyprus were about a hundred in number, and were under the command of Walter, Lord of Caesarea as early as 1217, Constable of Cyprus from at least 1210 to as late as 1220. He was killed June 24, 1229 before Nicosia while fighting for John d'Ibelin against the partisans of Emperor Frederick.

made an attack from the side. The Italian foot soldiers fled first, after them horsemen of various nations, and certain Hospitallers of Saint John, while the Legate of the Roman See, and the Patriarch, who was carrying the Cross, begged them earnestly to stand their ground, but in vain. The heat of the sun was intense, the foot soldiers were burdened with the weight of their arms. The difficulty of the way increased the heat, and those who had brought wine with them drank it unmixed in the distress of their thirst because of the lack of water. With all these things happening at the same time, those who defended themselves as they stood their ground and turned their backs on those who fled first in their breathless course were wiped out, collapsing without wounds. But the King, with the Templars, and the House of the Teutons, and the Hospitallers of Saint John, and the counts of Holland, and of Wied, of Saarbrücken and Chester, with Walter of Berthout,[3] several counts of France and of Pisa, and other knights, sustained the attack of the pursuers. The King was almost burned with Greek fire; these men all served as a protection for those who were fleeing. As often as they showed their faces to the enemy, so often did the enemy flee, but as they gradually returned, these men had to sustain the blows and weapons of the enemy.

Captured in that defense of Christianity were the Bishop-elect of Beauvais[4] and his brother;[5] the Chamberlain of France and his son;[6] the Viscount of Belmont and brother of the Bishop of Angers;[7] John of Arcis, a noble and vigorous

3. Walter III of Berthout, a noble of Brabant and Lord of Mechlin 1180-1219 (1220?).

4. The Bishop-elect of Beauvais was Milon of Chatillon-Neuilly, 1217-34, son of Gaucher, Lord of Chatillon-sur-Marne and of Helvis, Lady of Nanteuil. He left for the Orient on the news of the death of Alberic, Archbishop of Rheims, whose diocese he had been administering. He was not freed from the Saracens until 1222.

5. André of Nanteuil who had been among the "Chevaliers bannerets" under Philip Augustus.

6. The Chamberlain of France since 1205 had been Walter II of Villebéon, who died shortly after 1219 in the Holy Land. His son, Adam de Villebéon, became in his turn Chamberlain in 1223 and died in 1238.

7. The brother of William of Belmont (or Beaumont), Bishop of Angers, was probably Richard, Viscount of Belmont and Lord of Sainte-Suzanne, who died in battle at Gaza in 1239.

man;[8] Henry of Uelmen;[9] and many others who were massacred or taken into captivity. Thirty-three Templars were
captured or killed with the Marshal of the Hospital of Saint
John,[10] and certain other brothers of the same House. Nor
did the House of the Teutons escape without loss. The army
of the Temple, which is usually first to assemble, was last to
retreat. Therefore, when it arrived last at our ramparts, it
stayed without, so that it might bring those who were before
it back within the walls as soon as it was possible. Our persecutors finally returned to lead off the captives and to gather
their spoils, presenting, as we afterwards learned from a Saracen, five hundred heads of Christians to the Sultan. Gloom
took possession of our men, but not despair. For we know
that this affliction was the punishment of sin, and that there
was less in the punishment than our fault demanded, since
He tempered the chastisement Who says to the soul of the
sinner, "Thou hast prostituted thyself to many lovers; nevertheless return to me, and I will receive thee."[11] But it is clear
to us that the unbelievers sustained grievous losses in their
own picked army. That day "was the day of our tribulation,
and of divine rebuke."[12] Truly the Lord is merciful Who
"does not forget to show mercy, and in His anger will not
shut up His mercies, Who in time of tribulation forgiveth sins;
Who commanded light to shine out of darkness; Who turns
our mourning into joy,"[13] our sorrow into gladness. For the

8. John of Arcis is referred to by Alberic des Trois Fontaines as Joannes de
Arceis, and by the chronicle of Liége as de Archi. He had with him an
illegitimate son, André of Espeissis. The father had been with King Philip
at the battle of Bouvines. He fought so bravely at the tower that he was
called *Berris*, probably a corruption of the Arabic *Bariz*, "a warrior more
brave than others."
   9. Henry had already been on the crusades at the taking of Constantinople, and had taken home many stolen relics.
   10. The Marshal of the Hospital was Aymar de Layron, who had been lord
of Caesarea, 1193–1213, by marriage with Julianne, Lady of Caesarea. He
entered the hospital, probably at the death of Julianne, and appears as
Marshal thereof during the Fifth Crusade. Although Oliver's statement is
ambiguous, we may assume that Aymar was killed at this time as he never
appears thereafter.
   11. Jeremias 3:1.
   12. IV Kings 19:3.
   13. Psalms 76:9; Tobias 3:13; II Corinthians 4:6; Esther 13:17.

Sultan, sending one of our captives, began to negotiate with us concerning peace or a truce, during which negotiation we promptly repaired our ramparts and other fortifications.

Chapter 30

Meanwhile the sailors, who were betrayers of Christianity, and with them very many pilgrims whose love of themselves was greater than their compassion for their brethren, before the time of the accustomed passage, left the soldiers of Christ in the greatest danger; hoisting their sails and leaving port, they afforded dejection to us and courage to the Babylonians.

Interrupting our arrangement of peace on the vigil of Saints Cosmas and Damian and on the following feast day [Sept. 26–28] and even on the next Saturday, with galleys and barbots on the river, and with mangonels,[1] shields, and tree-trunks for filling in the ditch on land, they attacked us with their usual barbaric ferocity and violence. But the Mighty Warrior, the "Triumpher in Israel,"[2] using His customary kindness, defended His camp, sending Savary of Mauléon[3] over the sea with armed galleys and very many warriors in this crisis of distress; and we, crying out to heaven, did not hesitate to rush into battle, but manfully stood our ground, killing, and forcing the emeny, wounded and confused, to withdraw from his three-day attack by the power of Him Who saves those who trust in Him.

Chapter 31

Meanwhile the city, being grievously afflicted by the long siege, by sword, famine, and pestilence, even more than can

1. A military engine used formerly for throwing stones, javelins, etc.
2. I Kings 15:29.
3. Savary of Mauléon, in Poitou, son of Ralph de Mauléon, helped the Count of Toulouse in the quarrel between France and England. Later he served in the English army. In 1224 he helped defend La Rochelle against Louis VIII. Finally he made homage to the French king, and was made governor of the islands near La Rochelle. He resisted the regent during the minority of St. Louis and died in 1233. He was also a celebrated poet, but not of any great ability, according to the *Histoire Littéraire de la France,* XVIII (Paris, 1895), p. 671.

be written, placed its hope solely in the peace which the Sultan had promised the citizens. For famine had grown so strong in it that desirable foods were lacking, although spoiled foods abounded. For the grain of Egypt is not lasting on account of the soft earth in which it grows, except in the higher lands around Babylon where it is skillfully preserved for years; and as we heard, one fig was sold there for eleven besants. Because of the distress of the famine, various kinds of diseases harassed them; among the other grievances which they suffered, they were said to see nothing at night, as if struck by blindness, though their eyes were open. The Sultan, dissuading them from surrender, deceived the wretched men from day to day by empty promises. Finally, however, they blockaded their gates from within so that no one, coming to us from their number, might tell us how the days of affliction beset them. But any who could escape through the postern gate or down the walls by ropes clearly proved the distress of their people by their swollen and famished condition. The supply of bread and fodder began to diminish even for those who were besieging us from without in the army of the Saracens. For the Nile, which usually overflows from after the feast of Saint John the Baptist [June 24] until the Exaltation of the Holy Cross [Sept. 14] and irrigates the plains of Egypt, did not rise this year according to its custom to the mark which the Egyptians usually place, but, as we learned, left a great part of the land dry, which could not be ploughed or sown at the proper season. Therefore the Sultan fearing dearth and famine, and also because of his desire to keep Damietta, offered the Christians a peace with Coradin his brother on these terms: that he would give back the Holy Cross[1] which had formerly been captured in the victory of Saladin, along with the Holy City and all the captives who could be found alive throughout the kingdom of Babylon and Damascus, and also funds to repair the walls of Jerusalem; in addition he would restore the kingdom of Jerusalem entirely,

1. The crusaders often carried a relic of the Cross into battle. Many complained that Baldwin II endangered its safety by dangerous expeditions. It was lost by the Christians in the crushing defeat at the Horns of Hattin, July 4, 1187, but another part remained in the hands of the Christians.

except Krak and Montréal,[2] for the possession of which he would offer tribute for as long as the truce would last.

Now these are two places located in Arabia, which have seven very strong fortresses through which merchants of the Saracens and of the pilgrims, going to Mecca or returning from it, usually cross; and whoever holds them in his power can very seriously injure Jerusalem with her fields and vineyards when he wishes. The King and the French and the Count of Chester with the leaders of the Germans firmly believed that this arrangement was of advantage to Christianity, and ought to be accepted; and it was not to be marveled at, since they would have been satisfied with the much more insignificant peace which was formerly offered, had they not been opposed by wise counsel. But the Legate, with the Patriarch, the archbishops and bishops, the Templars and Hospitallers, and all the leaders of Italy[3] and many other prudent men, effectively resisted this arrangement, showing reasonably that Damietta ought to be taken before everything. Difference of opinion produced discord which was quickly settled because of the common need. Meanwhile the Sultan secretly sent a great multitude of foot soldiers through the marshy places to the city on the Sunday night after the feast of All Saints [Nov. 2–3]; two hundred and forty of them attacked the palisades while the Christians were sleeping; but the outcry of the sentries roused us, and about two hundred or more, according to our count, were killed or captured.

Chapter 32

On November fifth, in the reign of the Savior of the world, and with Pelagius, Bishop of Albano, skillfully and vigilantly

2. The castles of Krak and Montréal were located in the desert east of the Dead Sea. They commanded the caravan route between Syria and the south and were a constant menace to the Moslems when held by Christians. It was from them that Renaud de Chatillon had waged his campaigns against Saladin in the 1170's and 1180's. These fortresses had been a thorn in the flesh of the Moslems since their construction under Baldwin I, and they had no intention of ever letting them fall into Christian hands again.

3. The Italians had their minds fixed upon the commercial advantages which would result to Pisa, Genoa, and Venice from possession of the delta by Europeans. Hence their opposition to the lifting of the siege of Damietta. Oliver's partisanship for Pelagius is evident in his treatment of this episode.

executing the office of Legate of the Apostolic See, Damietta was captured without treachery, without resistance, without violent pillage and tumult, so that the victory may be ascribed to the Son of God alone, Who inspired His people to the entrance of Egypt and administered help there. And when the city was captured before the eyes of the King of Babylon, he did not dare, according to his usual custom, to attack through our rampart the soldiers of Christ who were prepared for the attack. At the same time also the river overflowed, filling our ditch with copious water. But the Sultan himself, in confusion, burned his own camp and fled. But God, Who on the third day gathered the waters under the firmament into one place, Who Himself brought His soldiers through the waters of the sea to the harbor of Damietta on the third day of the month of May, led them over the Nile to besiege the city on the third day of the month of February, and Himself captured Damietta located amidst the waters, on the third day of the month of November.

We can liken this city, which was overthrown by a third shaking of the earth, to a destroying bull; we call it "bull" because of its wantonness. For because of its fishes, birds, and pastures, grain, gardens, and orchards, it grew rich by trading and by practising piracy. It has overflowed with delights in its guilt, it has overflowed in hell. "But in one hour has thy judgment come."[1] We say "destroying" because its inhabitants perished in the third shaking of the earth, yet it remained unharmed itself. It was first besieged by the Greeks and Latins who finally went away from it;[2] next by the Latins under Amalric, King of Jerusalem, who were not successful;[3] but this third time, the "King of kings and Lord of lords"[4] delivered it to His servants; Jesus Christ, Who conquers and reigns and commands, "Who for the Egyptians has dried up everything sown by the water, and hath confounded them

1. Apocalypse 18:10.
2. In the autumn of 1169 Constantinople supplied many ships for King Amalric I (1162-74) and his army. Shortage of food and bad weather helped to terminate the unsuccessful siege in December of the same year.
3. Oliver is confused on these campaigns. The Greeks and Amalric were together in the siege of 1169 (*see* preceding note). Amalric's earlier campaigns took place in 1163 and 1167.
4. Apocalypse 19:16.

that wrought in flax and silk, combing and weaving fine cloth."[5] With this Leader, the soldiers of Christ, attacking Damietta, found its streets strewn with the bodies of the dead, wasting away from pestilence and famine; very much gold and silver, silk stuffs of the merchants in abundance, various household goods in superabundance. In addition to the natural location of the place, by which it is fortified, this city is surrounded by a triple wall, stoutly protected by many large brick towers; it is the key to all Egypt, and its protection is well located between Raamses and the field of Tanis in the land of Gessen,[6] as we can surmise because there is the pasture land which the sons of Israel sought from Pharaoh at the time of famine.[7]

Chapter 33

Damietta! renowned among kingdoms, very famous in the pride of Babylon, ruler of the sea, plunderer of Christians, seized in the pride of your persecutors by means of a few small ladders, now you are "humbled under the mighty hand of God";[1] and casting out the adulterer whom you kept for a long time, you have returned to your former husband; and you who first brought forth bastards, now shall bear legitimate sons for the faith of the Son of God, being firmly held by the faithful of Christ. The Bishop of Acre[2] released from you the first fruits of souls for God by cleansing in the sacramental waters of baptism your little ones, who were found in you, alive by His power, even though they were near death. You have been subjected to manifold punishments because besides those who were taken alive in you, your dead of both sexes from the time of the siege round about you are computed at thirty thousand and more. The Lord struck them down without sword and fire, scorning henceforth to endure the uncleanness comitted in you.

5. Isaias 19:7-9.
6. This is inaccurate, for both Raamses and Tanis are south of Damietta.
7. *See* Genesis 47.

1. I Peter 5:6.
2. Jacques de Vitry is portrayed as doing the same at Mount Tabor.

Chapter 34

Therefore let the universal Church rejoice by returning worthy acts of thanksgiving for such a triumph, and not only for Damietta, but for the destruction of the dangerous fortress of Mount Tabor and for our free approach into Jerusalem, that its walls may be rebuilt at the time foreseen by the Most High; besides, for the Castle of the Son of God, which the army of the Temple, at great expense, is making useful and impregnable, concerning which we have written more fully above. Rejoice, province of Cologne, exult and give praise, because in ships, instruments of war, warriors and weapons, supplies and money, you have given more aid than the rest of the entire German kingdom! Our illustrious Emperor and King of Sicily is being eagerly awaited by the people of God for the happy consummation of the enterprise. Thou, O Cologne, city of saints, who dwellest in the gardens of the roses of martyrs, of the lilies of virgins, of the violets of confessors,[1] now rejoicing in a temporal peace through our venerable Archbishop, because of the devotion of thy daughters, bend the knees of thy heart before the Most High, Who has power of life and death. "Be not high minded, but in His sight fear, reprove your ways, lest the wrath of God which hath fallen upon thee"[2] be turned into hail, but . . . since peaceful times have long been granted, serve Him with a free mind, to Whom is honor and excellence, might and power.[3]

Chapter 35

Before the capture of Damietta there came to our attention a book written in Arabic, in which the author says that he was

1. *See* Canticle of Canticles 6:1-2.
2. Romans 11:20; Job 13:15; II Paralipomenon 34:21.
3. Five manuscripts give this reading, instead of the words "Our illustrious Emperor," etc.: "But you, Cologne, city of saints, who dwell in gardens among the lilies of virgins, the roses of martyrs, the violets of confessors, bend the knees of your heart for the devotion of your daughters, and intone glorious acts of thanksgiving in lofty words."

neither Jew nor Christian nor Saracen. But whoever he was, he predicted the evils which Saladin curelly brought upon the Christian people in the destruction of Tiberias, and in the victory which he had over the Christians when he took captive the King of Jerusalem and its princes, occupied the Holy City, and destroyed Ascalon; it also predicted how he tried to seize Tyre but did not succeed, and many other things which the sins of that time deserved.[1] He also foretold the destruction of the gardens of the palm grove of the city of Damietta, which we saw had been accomplished when we examined this book through an interpreter. He also added that Damietta would be captured by the Christians; he does not use the name of Saladin, but points him out by means of his black eyes and saffron banners. Besides, he predicted that a certain king[2] of the Christian Nubians was to destroy the city of Mecca and cast out the scattered bones of Mohammed, the false prophet, and certain other things which have not yet come to pass. If they are brought about, however, they will lead to the exaltation of Christianity and the suppression of the Agarenes.[3] We know that certain heathen gentiles had the Holy Spirit on their lips, but not in their

1. The prophecies themselves may be read in *Quinti Belli Sacri Scriptores Minores*, II, ed. Röhricht (Genevae, 1879), where they are given as *Le Prophétie de Hannan* (pp. 206-13), and *Prophetia Filii Agap* (pp. 214-28).

2. A legendary Eastern priest and king of the race of the Magi was Prester John, often referred to by late medieval historians. The first authentic mention of him is made in 1145 by Otto of Freising in his Chronicle. When Damietta was conquered in 1221, the victors spread a report that in the East, King David, either the son or the nephew of Prester John, had started with three strong armies against the Mohammedans. An Arabic prophecy foretold that Islam would be abolished when Easter fell on April 3. When this happened in 1222, many thought that King David (referred to here by Oliver) and his forces would join the expected army of Frederick II. Enthusiasm over this hope helped lead to the premature outbreak against Cairo and the defeat of the crusaders. The origin of the name David has not been satisfactorily explained, but the story has an historical kernel in that about this time Jenghiz Khan led three groups and destroyed the Mohammedan power in inner Asia.

3. The Saracens were often referred to as Agarenes during the Middle Ages. Marbury B. Ogle, "Petrus Comestor, Methodius and the Saracens," *Speculum* XXI (1946), 318-24, points out that the tradition of ecclesiastical historians, influenced by St. Jerome's rendering of the Chronicle of Eusebius, very often referred to Saracens as Agarenes because of their reputed descent from Agar, the handmaid of Abraham.

heart, and prophesied plainly about Christ; therefore we are not surprised if purer water flows through stone channels. Besides this, a report, spreading through the whole world, that Damietta had been captured by the Christians, caused a letter of the Georgians to be sent to the camp of the Catholics. It said that that nation, angered and roused by shame, decreed and swore, as the king convoked the leaders, that she would besiege some famous city of the Saracens, alleging that she would be ashamed because the Franks, coming from regions across the sea, and from the uttermost bounds of the earth, over a vast ocean full of dangers, had captured so well fortified a city by a long siege, unless they themselves, for whom it was easier to attack the enemy, should capture Damascus, or another specified place, by the strength of their arms. Now the Georgians are believers in Christ, and are neighbors to the Persians, separated from the Land of Promise by a long stretch of country; their kingdom extends as far as the Caspian Mountains, on which ten tribes enclosed (there) await the time of anti-Christ, for then they will burst forth and will cause great destruction. The Georgians are warlike men, having the tonsure on their heads, round for the clergy, and square for the laity. Their women of the noble class are trained for battle. When those men are going to attack the enemy in orderly array, each one drinks a small gourd filled with pure wine, and at once they attack their adversaries courageously.

We do not doubt that it is to be counted among the favors of Christ our Protector, that He defended our leaders from the murderers of our persecutors in the siege of Damietta. For the Assassins[4] and their chief, the Old Man of the Mountains,[5] had the custom of casting knives against the Christians

4. The Secret order of Assassins had been founded by a Persian named Hassan late in the 11th century. Though they originally killed the enemies of their brand of Islam, they later killed for political reasons and made themselves feared throughout the East. Their first location was Alamut, near the Caspian Sea, but they later gained a series of fortresses in Lebanon.

5. The leader of the Assassins was known to the Christians as the Old Man of the Mountains. His power was very extensive, for he had at his disposal a fanatical band of experts in murder. Even Saladin felt compelled to treat with him. As the Old Man was supposed to live forever and the elections to

to cut off the lives of those who care for the business of Christianity. For at the time of the truce they wantonly killed the son of the Count of Tripoli,[6] a fine young man, who was prostrate before the altar in the church of the Blessed Virgin at Tortosa; wherefore the army of the Temple did not cease to pursue them for such a violation of religious liberty, until they were humiliated to the servitude of paying a tribute of three thousand besants annually to the Templars.

Chapter 36

At the time of the siege, Leo, King of Armenia, died at a good old age.[1] Likewise the Sultan of Iconium[2] died. He is believed to have been baptized, and was so kindly disposed toward the Christians that when making war on the side of the Saracens he ordered the followers of Christ to be released whom he found in chains in the fortification which he attacked. He gave them their choice of returning into their own country, if they wished, or of receiving money from him and waging war under him if they preferred. So familiar was he with Christians, that he made them guardians of his own

the office were held in the greatest secrecy, the names of but few of these rulers are known.

6. Bohemond IV, the One-Eyed, was first Regent, then (from 1199) Count of Tripoli. By his first wife, Plaisance of Gibelet, he had a son Raymond who is here referred to.

1. Leo II, the Great, 1187 (crowned 1189)-1219. With the help of the Hospitallers he had dispossessed 'Izz-al-Dîn I of Iconium of the cities of Heraclea and Laranda in southeast Cappadocia in 1211. When John of Brienne in 1212 lost his first wife, Marie of Montferrat, Leo's daughter Stephanie was given to him in marriage.

2. 'Izz-al-Dîn Kaikâwus I, a Seljuk, Sultan of Iconium, 1210-19. In 1216 he took full revenge on Leo for the loss of Laranda by crushing the Armenian army under the Constable Constantine and capturing the leader along with many Armenian nobles. To ransom these captives, Leo had not only to restore Laranda, but also to cede the region of Bozanti and Ermaneksu in Isauria. Sultan 'Ala-al-Dîn Kaîqubâd I (1219-37), his successor, took from the Armenians all the rest of Isauria except Selefke. The mistaken belief that some Mohammedan leaders were ready for conversion made Oliver write in 1221 a letter to the "King of Babylon" urging him to become a Christian and another to the "Doctors of Egypt" at the same time.

person, although his father had been killed by Lascaris the Greek.[3] He also supported Miralis,[4] the disinherited son of Saladin, against the sons of Saphadin, as far as the Caliph of Baghdad, pope of his own race, permitted.

Melchiseraph,[5] son of Saphadin, inflicted many losses on the Templars when they were in the siege of Damietta; for he burned the town of Safita,[6] and destroyed its fortified towers. But when he returned to his own land, he was conquered by the Saracens. At the same time Bohemond, Count of Tripoli, attacking Antioch, forcibly ejected Rupen, a certain kinsman of his, from the rule of that city,[7] choosing rather to have the pleasure of a temporal sin than to be afflicted along with the Christian people. Therefore the Legate of the Apostolic See officially proclaimed the sentence of excommunication and interdict against him and Tripoli and the lands in which he committed the crime.

Chapter 37

"The Lord hath broken the staff of the wicked. He hath broken the horn of the proud; He Who above the sons of men

3. In the spring of 1211 Theodore Lascaris killed Sultan Kaîkhosru of Iconium in battle.

4. When Saladin died in 1186, his oldest son, Malik-al-Afdal (known to the Latins as Miralis), succeeded him at Damascus, in southern Syria, and in Palestine. In 1196 he was overthrown by his uncle, Saphadin, who also seized the throne of Egypt in 1200 from another nephew, Malik-al-'Aziz.

5. Malik-al-Aschraf, son of Saphadin, helped overthrow his nephew Al-Malik en-Nasser Salah-ed-Dîn Dawoud in 1228, and succeeded him at Damascus. He died August 27, 1237.

6. Safita, or Chastel-Blanc, is southeast of Tortosa. In Chapter 42 of Oliver, Coradin (Al-Malik al-Moadden), son of Saphadin, is rightly mentioned as its destroyer. The place was known to Greek writers as Argyrokastron, and belonged to the Templars. Saladin gained possession of it before he died, and Coradin demolished it, as mentioned here, in 1219 or 1220. It was again fortified by the Templars in 1246 or 1247, and was finally conquered by Baibars in 1271.

7. Bohemond IV, the One-Eyed, with the aid of Templars, seized the rule of Antioch from his nephew Rupen-Raymond, the son of his older brother and the daughter of Leo of Armenia. Leo championed his grandson. Twice Rupen was installed in Antioch by Armenian arms, but he was finally driven out, and died trying to assert his claims to the throne of Armenia.

is terrible,"[1] has powerfully opened the gate of Damietta. As
we were entering it, there met us an intolerable odor, a
wretched sight. The dead killed the living. Man and wife,
father and son, master and slave, killed each other by their
odor. Not only were the streets full of the dead, but in the
houses, in the bedrooms, and on the beds lay the corpses.
When a husband had perished, a woman, powerless to rise
and lacking the help of one to support her, died, not being
able to bear the odor; a son near his father or vice versa, a
handmaid beside her mistress or vice versa, wasted away
with illness and lay dead. "Little ones asked for bread and
there was none to break it for them,"[2] infants hanging at the
breasts of their mothers opened their mouths in the embrace
of one dead. Fastidious rich men died of hunger amid piles
of wheat, those foods being lacking by which they had been
raised; in vain did they desire melons and garlic, onions, fish
and fowl, fruits of the tree and herbs. In them was fulfilled
the prophecy of the prophet: "Instead of a sweet smell there
shall be stench, as rotten carcass shall not have company in
burial."[3] Almost eighty thousand, as we learned from the
report of captives, perished in the city from the beginning of
the siege to its end; all except those whom we found, healthy
or ill, about three thousand in number. Three hundred of
these, the more notable ones of both sexes, were kept for the
ransom of our captives; some died after the victory, others
were sold for a great price, and others were baptized and
given to Christ.

Chapter 38

This city fortified in degrees had its first wall low for the
protection of the ditch, the second one higher, the third
loftier than the second. The middle wall has twenty-eight
main towers containing two or three tortoises[1] each, which

1. Isaias 14:5; Psalms 74:11; 65:5.
2. Lamentations 4:4.
3. Isaias 3:24; 14:19-20.

1. A sort of penthouse under which fighters were protected, as a tortoise
by its shell.

all remained unharmed along with the walls, except one which was considerably shattered by the frequent blows of the trebuchet of the Duke of Austria. For our army was so given over to dissipation that the knights devoted themselves to leisure, neglecting the work of God, while the common people turned to the taverns and to fraudulent dealings. Two cats[2] had been made at great expense to fill the ditch. One of them in the custody of the King, the other in the custody of the Romans, were burned when the guardians of the city were sill powerful in arms. Two subterranean ditches were made to undermine the foundations of the fortifications; but that labor was frustrated after very much expense. The Lord wished to give the city unharmed, without loss of those capturing it, and that by reason of His power. We all swore in common that the spoils carried off from the city should be given up to be divided among the victors; this also was enjoined under terrible anathema by the Legate of the Apostolic See. Transgressors will remain to be reckoned in disgrace forever with Achan,[3] who at Jericho took something of what had been anathematized. Truly the concupiscence of the eyes made many men thieves. Nevertheless we received for the benefit of the state a great part of the luxuries of Egypt, in gold and silver, pearls and apples of amber, golden threads and various fringes, precious silken stuffs, as Isaias enumerates: "In that day he will take away the ornaments of shoes, and little moons, and chains and necklaces, and bracelets and bonnets, and bodkins and ornaments of the legs, and tablets and sweet balls and earrings, and rings and jewels hanging on the forehead, and changes of apparel, and short cloaks and fine linen and crisping pins, and looking-glasses, and lawns and headbands, and fine veils,"[4] which no one could list in full. But we are spending much time in considering them. These things were distributed through the army of the Lord with grain which was found in the city.

2. A kind of low movable defensive structure used in medieval warfare in approaching fortifications. Called also cat house, cat castle, and rat.

3. See Josue 7.

4. Isaias 3:18-23.

Chapter 39

The Legate of the Apostolic See joined Damietta, with all her dependents and belongings, to the Kingdom of Jerusalem forever. The mosque of Damietta, through the invocation of the holy and undivided Trinity, was converted into a church of the blessed and glorious Virgin Mary. Being built in square form, we can see almost as much of its width as we can of its length. It is supported by one hundred and forty-one marble columns, having seven porticoes, and in the middle a long wide-open space in which a pyramid ascends on high in the manner of a ciborium; beyond the west side a tower rises after the manner of a campanile. Four main altars are built in it: the first under the title of Blessed Mary; the second of Peter, the Prince of the Apostles; the third of the Holy Cross; the fourth of blessed Bartholomew, on whose feast the tower in the river was captured.

In Damietta were found four trebuchets with petraries and many mangonels; very strong ballistae with a lathe; on account of the multitude we do not know the number of hand ballistae and bows. Every kind of equipment for brave men that was found was kept for Christianity. Gold and silver, with pearls and other things easy to move, were divided proportionally not only among clerics and knights, but also among attendants, women, and children. The towers of the city with its homes were distributed among the kingdoms whose warriors had assembled for its capture; one tower was in the first place reserved, as was right and fitting, and was assigned to the Roman Church, with its gate, which formerly was called the Babylonian but now is called the Roman. Another tower also was reserved for the Archbishop of Damietta; and as formerly Jerusalem, the Holy City of the living God, was captured by the enemy at night, so the Christians obtained Damietta before dawn. The machine by which the tower of the river had been captured, the Germans and Frisians donated in common, and out of it was made a new bridge between the city and the fort which is constructed as a defense of the bank opposite the city. Two small fortresses were placed together for the protection of the bridge, by the same machine. Besides, from other trees on which the ladders hung, a watch place was set up on the summit of the new fort to point out the harbor to those sailing at a distance. An old bridge, which with an island in the middle touched both banks, had been attacked many times by the Saracens at the time of siege, and had been manfully defended by the Christians. Having done its work, it is kept for other uses.

Chapter 40

By no less a miracle, but rather by a greater one did the Lord give to the Christians the fort of Tanis,[1] in the month of November, on the feast of blessed Clement [Nov. 23] who has his dwelling on the sea. For scouts were sent, about a thousand in number, in small ships through the little river which is called the Tanis, so that they might take food supplies for themselves from the casalia and carefully explore the location of the aforesaid place. The Saracens, who were in the garrison of the fort, seeing the Christians and thinking that the whole army was arriving, fled after locking the doors. But our men, having Christ alone as their leader there, breaking through the barriers, entered the fort. Returning they declared to us that never had they seen a stronger fort on a plain; it had seven very strong towers, fortified by tortoises, and a breastwork; and besides it was surrounded by a twofold ditch, each part of which is protected by a wall. A lake stretches out in breadth round about to such an extent that approach is impossible to our horsemen in winter, and so difficult in summer that it would never be taken by our army in siege. The lake abounds in fish, and from its fisheries four thousand silver marks were paid annually to the Sultan of Babylon, as was told to us by elders; besides, it abounds in birds and salt works; many casalia round about were subject to it. The city beyond the fort, greater than Damietta, once

1. The biblical Taphnis, near Pelusium at the eastern border of Lower Egypt.

famous but now in ruins, bears witness to the size of its buildings. This is Tanis, whose field the prophet mentions: "Wonderful things did he do in the sight of their fathers,"[2] and Isaias: "Many princes of Tanis, the wise counselors of Pharaoh, have given foolish counsel."[3] This is Tanis, in which Jeremias is said to have been stoned. For when Jerusalem had been destroyed by the Babylonians,[4] and Godolias had been killed by Ishmael,[5] the rest of the people against the counsel of Jeremias set out into Egypt, taking with them Jeremias, who remained with them in Tanis, "and the word of the Lord was made known to Jeremias in Tanis: 'Take great stones and hide them in the vault that is under the brick wall at the gate of Pharaoh's house,' "[6] etc. Afterwards Jeremias said to them: "Thus sayeth the Lord: I have sworn by My great Name . . . that all the men of Juda that are in the land of Egypt shall perish by sword and by famine until they be wholly consumed."[7] And the people rose against Jeremias, and they stoned him with the stones which had been hidden under the brick wall. But the Egyptians honored the prophet, burying him next to the tomb of their kings, being mindful of the benefits which he had shown to Egypt. For by his words he had driven away the beasts of the waters, which the Greeks call crocodiles. Now Alexander the Macedonian, coming to the tomb of the prophet and being acquainted with the mystery of the place, transferred him to Alexandria and buried him gloriously.[8] But we found and killed crocodiles at Damietta. Now this beast is cruel, devouring men and animals, and it cares for its eggs simply by watching them with its eyes open. Its young, being hatched, flee the parent as an enemy; for in an instant it gulps down and devours whomever it can snatch.

2. Psalms 77:12.
3. Isaias 19:11.
4. *See* Jeremias 52.
5. Jeremias 41.
6. Jeremias 43:8-9.
7. Jeremias 44:26-27.
8. There is no mention of this in Curtius Rufus. Nothing certain is known about the last days of Jeremias. A Christian tradition states that he was stoned at Taphnis. It seems to begin with Tertullian.

Tanis is separated from Damietta by a journey of one day over the sea in the direction of the Land of Promise, so that it is easy to place a garrison there or to send food from Acre or from Damietta, across the sea or over land or by river. It caused many losses to the Christians in the siege of Damietta, when ships approaching us or going away from us were carried there by the force of the winds. For before Tanis, the coast, which is curved and without harbors, makes a wife, full bay; and ships drifing into it cannot withdraw without a wind that is highly favorable to them.

Chapter 41

Coradin, having returned from Egypt into Palestine, besieged the castle of Caesarea, which was in the custody of the King, and in a short time he captured and destroyed it while its defenders acted negligently; nevertheless they almost all escaped because they had a free entrance and exit over the sea. Next he proceeced to the Castle of the Son of God with all his army, and regarding it from every direction, he shrewdly realized that it could not be seized; besides he found the Templars prepared for every danger; for they had reinforced the camp with provisions and with all the equipment of brave men. At the same time the Templars manfully drove back the bandits of the Saracens from Acre by killing some and capturing others. But Coradin demanded help from the Saracens, so that coming from the east they might besiege Acre, a thing which he could not accomplish because of the constant discord of the princes of the land themselves, which was highly favorable to the Christians, and which the Caliph, their pope, labored to quiet.

Chapter 42

In the year of the Incarnate Word 1220, Coradin, Prince of Damascus, destroyed Safita.[1] Now this was the strongest fort of the Templars, which Saladin, the scourge of the Christians,

1. Here Oliver corrects his error of Chapter 36.

reduced by a long siege to such a point that the defenders, wasting away with hunger, and having obtained the permission of the Master of the army of the Temple, surrendered it to the tyrant. What voice, what tongue can repeat for us the benefits of our Savior, multiplied without us? They are benefits of Him Whom an inherent goodness and natural clemency, and also the continued supplication of the church, have induced to look with a kindly eye upon the camp of the faithful because of the sweetness of their devotion! A plea softens Him, a tear forces Him, and how can the hand of a writer or the tongue of a speaker be sufficient for Him for Whose praise a conscience remaining quiet in the heart is not sufficient? However, it is pleasing to heap up and admire the marvels wrought in a short space of time which descended from the Father of Lights. The sons of Israel were at hand, going about with the ark of the Lord, sounding their sackbuts and shouting, on the seventh day, when the walls of Jericho fell, so that the people of the Lord might have free entrance.[2] But we slept before Damietta, cowardly and sluggish, benumbed and given ever to idleness; none the less, the walls of Jerusalem fell, and those of Mount Tabor, Safita, and the other fortifications opposing in a hostile way; besides, the Most High, against the will of certain false Christians, gave us Damietta. To this, from the treasure of His generosity He added the impregnable fort of Tanis with its supply of provisions in a hostile land—He Who rained manna from heaven upon His believers in the desert. It is therefore clear to all, through the evidence of miracle, that this holy pilgrimage is pleasing and acceptable to God. May they blush and be confounded who received the rewards of the Supreme King from His Church, and, fighting indifferently or retreating before time, corrupted His pilgrimage; they will give an account to the Judge Who cannot be either corrupted or deceived. Let the sluggish be aroused, who have not yet carried out their vow. For "it is ruin to a man to devour holy ones, and after vows, to retract."[3] What excuse will they offer on the day of tribulation and distress, who took away the labors

2. Josue 6:11-20.
3. Proverbs 20:25.

of others,[4] killing souls to which preachers of the truth have given life; who had regard for their own avarice and took the sign of the Cross from the shoulders of the wretched, whom they made transgressors of their vow? Let them also return to wisdom whom guilt accuses and conscience convicts of this, that by alleging false reasons of poverty and debility, they have cheated the religion of those who have been examined, because only the judgment of God is according to truth. But the defrauders of the alms which were collected for the aid of the Holy Land, because they have concealed their fault by lying to the Holy Ghost, shall perish and have their lot with Ananias and Saphira;[5] and with Judas, the most wicked thief and betrayer of his Lord, they shall be punished in hell because, though betrayers of Christianity, they kept for themselves the wages of fighting men, and gave their souls for transitory things. Cupidity has caused their theft and they are unmindful of Jerusalem our mother, who, lying prostrate on the ground, desires to be lifted up from her Babylonian captivity by those who are returning. Be consoled, "city of God, because nations from afar shall come to thee, and bearing gifts, shall adore the Lord in thee; they shall be cursed who despised thee, and they shall be condemned that have blasphemed thee. The blessed that built thee up shall rejoice. But thou shalt rejoice in they children, and blessed are all they that love thee and that rejoice in thy peace."[6]

Chapter 43

It happened when the year was changing, when kings usually set out to war, that John, King of Jerusalem, left the camp of the faithful.[1] He feigned many reasons for excusing himself

4. *See* Ezechiel 23:29.
5. Acts 5:9.
6. Tobias 13:10-18.

1. Probably at Easter, March 29. John had become constantly more irritated at the attitude of Pelagius. He used the affairs of Aremnia as a pretext; he had married Stephanie, daughter of Leo II who died in 1219. John wished to claim the throne for himself in the name of his wife. Oliver explains John's Aremnian aspirations in Chapter 45.

and promised a speedy return, but forgetful of the past, he turned to the future. When the Lord opened His hand and filled the port of Damietta with abundance of grain, wine, and oil, and when a numerous band of pilgrims and horses had been added so that there might be no grounds of excuse for setting out upon an affair so happily begun, there arrived in the sixth passage the archbishops of Milan,[2] and Crete, the bishops of Faenza,[3] and Reggio,[4] and messengers of Frederick the King, bearing letters with golden seals and announcing his arrival. There was present the Bishop of Brescia[5] and a copious army of Italy. But the Legate considered that by a great privilege of grace and by divine bounty everything had been sufficiently attended to that the process of negotiation required; and he was struck with sorrow because time was passing away uselessly, and such a great opportunity was lost. Therefore, assembling the leaders, he, first of all, and after him the Archbishop of Milan, and other bishops likewise, strove to urge an advance against the Sultan who had pitched his camp on the Nile one day's journey from Damietta. But the knights, after holding a deliberation, spoke against this exhortation, pretending this reason above all—that the King of Jerusalem was away by voluntary choice, and no other prince was present whom the people of different nations were willing to obey to lead out the people of God—and thus they agreed upon inactivity, from which evils were multiplied in the camp.

Chapter 44

In the month of July came Count Matthew of Apulia[1] with eight galleys, two of which were corsairs that he had cap-

2. Henry Septala, Archbishop of Milan, 1213-30.
3. The Bishop of Crete is unknown. The Bishop of Faenza was Roland, 1210-21.
4. Bishop Lando, 1216-34.
5. Albert Rezzato, 1213-28.

1. Matteo Gentile, referred to in a diploma of 1229 as *Matthaeus Gentilis comes Alesinae* (present day Lesina) *et civitatis capitaneus et magister jus-titiarius Apuliae et Terrae Laboris.* He had been placed in charge of Apulia by Emperor Frederick, at whose orders he came on the crusade.

tured as they were threatening the Christians on the sea
journey.

Chapter 45

Let the temerity of human presumption blush, which trusts
erroneously in its own strength or in the strength of others,
and clearly is very often confounded. This appeared in the
case of the aforesaid Count. A previous report announced his
arrival by frequent rumors, and, as if the negotiation would
proceed only through him, its progress was hindered by
delaying circumstances. But the memory of such great hope
perished with a crash. It was not due to the Count that the
hope was not carried through to its desired consequence,
because, as the Legate witnessed, his will was prompt and
the equipment which he had brought and which he afterwards added appeared magnificent to all and in complete
accord with military knowledge. Besides he made a sojourn
in the army that was useful and suitable to the position of
a soldier of Christ. But after he arrived at Damietta, the Legate took counsel with any nation that was then in the camp
who seemed to have the greatest zeal, and with Count
Matthew himself, to whom an advance against the King
of Babylon seemed advantageous. Next he called the princes
and leaders of the multitude, and in a public address roused
to labor a people who were sluggish and given over to idleness.

But the leaders, especially the Franks, spoke against this
honorable exhortation, effectively inducing the Earl of Arundel,[1] a leader among the English, and the more noble among
the Germans, to hinder the proposal of the Legate. Among
other trifling reasons, the absence of King John was frequently alleged, who had acted contrary to the agreement
which he had made at Acre when the pilgrims were about
to sail into Egypt, that he would not desert them while he
was alive and free. Contrary to his solemn agreement he

---

1. William, Earl of Arundel and Sussex. He was active in all the contests
between John Lackland and the French king. He died in Italy in 1220 or 1221
after his return from the crusade.

returned to Acre; and not attending to the business of Christianity, he prepared himself and made a journey to Armenia. For having as his wife the daughter of Leo, the deceased King of Armenia, he aimed at the dominion of that region, as it is said; but being frustrated in his hope, he was not received by the barons of Armenia. At almost the same time the Queen died, along with the King's little son. Rupen, Prince of Antioch, also sought this kingdom; a Catholicos,[2] primate of the aforesaid nation, powerfully besieged him in the city of Tarsus; he was taken and imprisoned, and died there. Now the Catholicos favored the younger daughter of King Leo,[3] to whom her father before his death made the princes of his kingdom swear fealty; he died a short time afterwards.

Chapter 46

The Legate, after frequent public and private admonitions, grieved that so numerous an army was stationary, and not progressing, and would be going back in the next passage; finally by his example of action, he began to urge others to join the retinue, causing his tents to be pitched in a flat place. However, the opposition of the leaders prevailed to such a degree that even some Gallic and German mercenaries, who had accepted his money, hindered his plan of advancing. Certain of them were excommunicated, and others who were to be excommunicated afterwards were disturbed, and

2. Catholicos is the title given to the heads of the Armenian, Georgian, and Nestorian churches. At first it designated a dignitary superior to a metropolitan, but inferior to a patriarch. Now the term means the same as patriarch usually, but present-day Armenians have three catholicoi and two patriarchs. The primacy of honor is given to the Catholicos of Etshmiadzin. The Catholicos at the time of Leo's death was John Medzabaro.

3. Zabel was daughter of Leo II by his second wife, Sybille, daughter of Aymeri de Lusignan, king of Cyprus. She married Philip, son of Bohemond IV of Antioch and of Plaisance of Gibelet. Philip was put to death in prison by order of the Grand-Baron Constantine whose son Hayton then married Zabel (1224-25). Hayton exercised little power until the death of his father. He abdicated in 1270, and entered a monastery where he took the name of Macarius (see Chapter 87).

were compelled to return the pay that they accepted according to proportion of time. The Italian soldiers by vain hope cheated the religious zeal of the Legate, promising assistance for the advance, "but the sons of Ephraim, bending and shooting the bow, have turned back in the day of battle."[1] For while they were clearly regarding the persistence of the Legate and the boldness of the march against the Sultan, they agreed with the dissenters mentioned above, and opposed the advance, although the Christians did not lack an abundance of soldiers or attendants. Galleys were in abundance, barbots were prepared, a numerous multitude of archers was present, there was a plentiful supply of provisions, there was a suitable place between the river on the right and the lake on the left, as if the Lord were saying to us: "What is there I ought to do more to my vineyard and I have not done it? Was it that I looked that it should bring forth grapes and it hath brought forth wild grapes?"[2] For besides the other things which were provided by the Lord for the setting out of the expedition, as we learned from our scouts, the King of Babylon then had little aid, and a great multitude of Bedouins had joined us and would have given their wives and children as hostages if they had known that the Christians had undertaken the attempt manfully, as we learned through their letters and messengers. And this seemed probable because they are subject under tribute to the Sultan; indeed they formerly ruled in the land of Egypt until they were powerfully oppressed by Saladin and were scattered through the wilderness of the desert.

Chapter 47

The Legate after much weariness, because he had an unwilling retinue and especially because the river overflowed at that time, withdrew to the previous camp, strongly urging the authors of the delay, in a public sermon, that the work

1. Psalms 77:9.
2. Isaias 5:4.

of God, being happily begun, should not be ended and that
they should judge themselves, lest they be grievously condemned by the Judge of secret things.

Chapter 48

No one can describe the corruption of our army after Damietta was given us by God, and the fortress of tanis was
added. Lazy and effeminate, the people were contaminated
with chamberings and drunkenness, fornications and adul-
teries, thefts and wicked gains. Afterwards,[1] certain of our
men set out for a day's march into hostile territory, bringing
back captives, oxen, and horses. Then the Templars, with
their own special following, advanced in a swift march to a
town on the seacoast, which is called Broil,[2] and brought back
many spoils—about one hundred camels, the same number
of captives, horses, mules, oxen, and asses and goats, clothing
and much household furniture, returning unharmed after
two days. However, on account of a lack of water, many
horses and mules died on the way, although the men themselves returned safe. The Teutonic House, with many others,
met them for joy, but when they delayed behind the Templars (it is not fully known for what reason), the swift horsemen of the Turks made an attack on them at the sea. Terrified men from other nations fled from them, but the
English, the Flemish, the Teutons, and Robert of Belmont[3]
sustained the attack as they came upon them. The Preceptor
and the Marshal of the same House, with many other brothers and about twenty secular knights, were captured. Many
horses of those who fled to defend themselves were killed
because our men went out, not for battle, but to meet the
Templars, and therefore were without crossbowmen and
archers.

1. In July 1220. This was, for the time, the only advance that Pelagius could
urge upon the army. Outside of this pillaging expedition, the army remained
inactive for the rest of 1220 and until June 1221.
2. Broil lies to the west of Damietta and is today called Burlus.
3. Apparently from a different Belmont (de Bello Monte) from that used
in the name of Viscount Richard (de Pulchro Monte).

Chapter 49

In the month of August there reached Damietta fourteen galleys equipped and sent at the same time by the Doge of Venice,[1] which brought some help to the Christians. At the same time the King of Babylon armed thirty-three galleys which caused us inestimable loss. For they captured the merchant ships, along with the men themselves, which were bringing supplies to Damietta; they even took the pilgrims captive, plundering and burning the ships. Besides, they attacked a large ship which was bringing Count Henry of Schwerin,[2] and other Teutonic nobles who were coming to us. They, however, defended themselves manfully; and having killed and wounded many pirates they fortunately escaped, although they lost one vessel from the Teutonic House, with barley which Greek fire destroyed.

Chapter 50

Here we are forced to insert the account of an unfortunate mishap. Count Diether of Katzenellenbogen[1] left us before the time of the passage with a great multitude of pilgrims, although he was strongly urged and admonished by the Lord Legate not to board that ship if he wished to set out for Thessalonica, but to go in a smaller vessel with a few men without diminishing the army. But he, with the master of the ship and many pilgrims, stubbornly took up the journey, and therefore, the Legate of the Apostolic See excommunicated that accursed ship and all who were sailing on it. Falling among pirates near Cyprus, it was burned. However, the

1. Pietro Ziani, Doge of Venice, 1205-29.
2. Henry I, the Lion; Duke of Saxony and Count of Schwerin, 1160-1227, known for his connection with the seizure of King Waldemar of Denmark in 1223. He was on the crusade from 1220, and had returned home by March 1222.

1. Diether II, Count of Katzenellenbogen, 1219-44, son of Diether I, 1214-19. He returned home in 1222.

shipwrecked Count escaped, swimming away with a few
men.

Chapter 51

The galleys of the Venetians and others being requested to
hurry, set out rather belatedly from the port of Damietta,
going to Rosetta and Alexandria after we had suffered losses
at the hands of the Saracens in the manner mentioned
above.

Chapter 52

Coradin, knowing our inactivity, gathered an army from
Syria, and more completely destroyed Jerusalem, the city of
the living God, though it had been destroyed before. He
scattered the cisterns that had previously been filled, had the
city's marble columns carried off to Damascus, and advancing through the mountains and fields of Palestine he laid
waste its fruit-bearing trees and vines. The Templars, knowing that he wished to besiege the Castle of the Son of God,
began to destroy the deserted tower of Destroit in the upper
section. But he, coming upon them later, razed it to the
ground, cutting down the fruitful garden placed before it; he
finally besieged the fort with a multitude of Turks, extending
the line of their tents from the river to the salt works. Now
he derived this audacity from the fact that he knew that
around the beginning of October the seventh passage had
been so small; for we believe that not one hundred soldiers
came to our aid then with military weapons and horses. But
a great multitude of the people of Acre came to Damietta,
being driven from their lands by the pronouncement of the
church. From that number those were allowed to return
whose poverty could be known to us; others returned without permission to the increase of their destruction; and still
others returned to their own lands after extorting permission
through fraud. But a few, who had a more rational attitude,
remained with us in exile.

Chapter 53

Coradin, having established the siege, and fearing an attack from the camp, ordered a rampart to be made between the fort and his tents. He set up one trebuchet, three petraries, and four mangonels, and harassed the fortification night and day by blows of the machines. However, he could not move one stone from its place in the new towers and the middle wall. But the trebuchet of the camp, with a petrary and a mangonel placed next to it, battered and broke the trebuchet and the petrary of the enemy. In the residence of the Templars, moreover, four thousand warriors were fed daily, except those who at their own expense had come from Acre to defend us or to sell provisions. But the Legate in haste requested the Queen of Cyprus[1] and the Christians, and the barons of Syria, through messengers and letters, to aid the fortress of Christianity. The Master of the Temple,[2] with a tested army of Templars, was permitted by the Legate, because of such a great need, to return to the Castle, and prepared to fight with Coradin. The men of Cyprus brought a great supply of soldiers and funds. Bohemond,[3] likewise, and the Lord of Beirut,[4] Guy of Gibelet,[5] with other pullani,[6] quickly prepared themselves to help. Learning this through

1. Alice, widow of Hugh of Lusignan. She was the daughter of Henry II, Count of Champagne, and Isabelle of Jerusalem.

2. Peter de Montagu, brother of Eustorgius of Nicosia and Guérin, Master of the Hospital, succeeded William of Chartres as Master of the Temple at the death of William in 1219. He held office until 1229.

3. Bohemond IV.

4. John d'Ibelin, lord of Beirut, 1177-1236, was the most influential baron in Jerusalem. He had been Regent of the kingdom, 1205-10, for his niece Marie (see J. L. LaMonte In *Byzantion* XII [1937], 417-48).

5. Guy of Gibelet (between Tyre and Beirut) was the son of Hugh II, Lord of Gibelet, and Etienette, daughter of Henry of Milly, brother of Philip, Lord of Naplouse. Guy's sister (by the same union) was Plaisance, wife of Bohemond IV, Prince of Antioch. Guy succeeded his father as Lord of Gibelet when he was still a minor. He married Alice, former wife of Bohemond. He survived the disaster of the crusade, and helped Frederick against the Ibelins in 1228 (see Chapter 87).

6. A name given the Syrian-born Franks. The term is sometimes used to refer to children of mixed Frankish-native alliances, but is more generally used, as here, to mean Franks native to Syria.

scouts and betrayers of the Christians, Coradin was struck with fear and basely withdrew from the siege, suffering great losses at the hands of those holding the Castle, both in men and in horses. Like a proud and arrogant man, he had threatened that he would take the Castle by a long siege; but divine power forced him to retreat after he burned his own camp around the beginning of November.

Now many of the defenders of the Castle were wounded and a few died. May the Most High protect this home, built to the honor of the Son of God, hateful to the Saracens, but lovely to the Christians, the breastwork of the city of Acre, as it were. May the custody of angels be upon its walls "even to the consummation of the world."[7] Truly, "we have faith in the Lord Jesus,"[8] since He Who began to destroy the enemies of the Cross is steadfast in His grace, and will accomplish it at the time of His own good pleasure. For already we perceived a certain proof of divine vengeance; for in the siege of the Castle, as we learned from our scouts, and clearly saw, since corpses were strewn through the fields, three emirs were killed there, and two hundred Mamelukes[9] most skilled in arms; but there was no count of their archers, and of those who were dragging them along in their machines, and who were destroyed by our crossbowmen, three hundred in number. In one day also were killed one hundred and twenty horses of great value, among which was one, bought for fourteen thousand drachmas, which Seraphus,[10] Sultan of Aleppo, sent to a certain emir for a gift; besides, the Saracens also sustained many losses of other horses and camels.[11]

7. Matthew 28:20.

8. *See* Ephesians 3:11-12.

9. Mamelukes were Turkish slaves purchased for service in the Army. The Egyptian dynasties that followed the Ayyubites are often called Mameluke dynasties, because the sultans were taken from the enfranchised slaves who made up the court and supplied officers to the Army.

10. Al-Malik al-Aschraf, son of Al-Adil, called Seraphus by European writers. He received from his father Edessa and Ayyubide Greater Armenia. In 1220 he became protector of the kingdom of Aleppo for Al-Aziz, whom he protected against the Seljuks of Anatolia.

11. *See* Appendix.

Chapter 54

In the month of November, Lord Frederick, son of the Emperor Henry,[1] was crowned Emperor in Rome under Pope Honorius, in the great harmony of state and priesthood, and in the peace of the Romans. Being signed with the Cross, he made ready to go to the assistance of the Holy Land, sending ahead the Duke of Bavaria,[2] who came to Damietta in the year 1221 in the eighth passage with the bishop of Passau,[3] the Marquis of Baden,[4] Count Guy of Brienne,[5] and other nobles in the month of May. The emperor committed his post to this leader until he should cross the sea in person. Then the Legate of the Apostolic See, considering the fitness of the time, and the cost of idleness, began to treat with the Duke again about the business of war, for the forwarding of which he had remained in Egypt. Besides, the aforesaid Duke urged that the multitude of the faithful should attack the camp of the Sultan, before the river should take up its usual increase. Therefore by the common plan of the barons, knights, and the common people we began to arrange tents up the river beyond the camp in the month of June on the feast of the apostles Peter and Paul [June 29]. It was known by the statement of the Bishop-elect of Beauvais and of others who are detained in captivity, and by the story of very many, that if the Legate had not been hindered by the opposition of those of whom we made mention above but, as he had ordered, had advanced against the Sultan before or after the swelling

1. Frederick II of Hohenstaufen, son of Henry VI and Constance of Sicily. He had been crowned King of Sicily and of Germany previously; this was his coronation as Emperor in Rome.
2. Ludwig of Wittelsbach, Duke of Bavaria, Count Palatine of the Rhine 1214-31. He took the Cross with Frederick in 1215.
3. Ulrich of Andechs-Dissen, Bishop of Passau since 1215, who died on the journey homeward on October 30, 1221. He had taken the Cross with Duke Ludwig of Bavaria in 1215.
4. Herman V, Marquis of Baden, brother of Henry I of Baden, 1212-31. Herman was back home by March 1222, and died in 1243.
5. According to Röhricht, this is Walter IV of Brienne, nephew of King John of Jerusalem. He married Marie of Cyprus, daughter of King Hugh I, became Count of Jaffa, and was killed fighting the Saracens in 1241.

of the river, then Egypt would have fallen to the lot of the Christians. For at that time the leaders of Egypt were disagreeing with the Sultan; and like Rahab the harlot, begging the kindness of God for her people, for herself, and for her house,[6] so the Egyptians sent presents and gifts to our captives in Cairo, begging that by means of them, they might find mercy at the hands of the victorious Christians. On the third day of the octave of the apostles [July 6], the Legate, beginning with a three days' fast, and assembling the clergy with the archbishops and bishops, carried barefoot the saving banner of the Cross in procession beyond Damietta to the camp located where the river rises. On the next day King John returned to Damietta, bringing a numerous following.

Chapter 55

"I will begin and I will make an end," saith the Lord. "Behold I shall make a word, and whosoever shall hear it both his ears shall tingle."[1] Mine is the dominion in the kingdoms of men, "My counsel shall stand, and all My will shall be done; there is no one who can resist My countenance. There is no wisdom, there is no prudence, there is no counsel against the disposition of My will. For the whole world before Me is as the least grain of the balance, and as a drop of the morning dew that falleth down upon the earth. Who shall say to Me, 'what hast Thou done?' or who shall withstand My judgment? I have found David My servant, with My holy oil I have anointed him"[2] king of the Indies, whom I have commanded to avenge My wrongs,[3] to rise against the many-headed beast, to whom I have given victory over the king of the Persians; I have placed a great part of Asia under his feet. The King of the Persians, being lifted up unto excessive

6. *See* Josue 2.

---

1. I Kings 3:11-12.
2. Isaias 46:10; Jeremias 49:19; Proverbs 21:30; Wisdom 11:23; 12:12; Psalms 88:21.
3. Probably a reference to Daniel 7.

pride, wished to be the monarch of Asia; against him King David,[4] who they say is the son of Prester John, won the first fruits of victory. Then he subjugated other kings and kingdoms to himself, and, as we learned by a report that reached far and wide, there is no power on earth that can resist him. He is believed to be the executor of divine vengeance, the hammer of Asia.

Chapter 56

Indeed after the capture of Damietta, the Legate of the Apostolic See had a book which was written in Arabic read aloud briefly and by means of an interpreter, in the hearing of the multitude; and as we considered and contemplated the antiquity of its bindings and maps, we discovered we ought to proceed. This book is entitled "The Book of Clement,"[1] written as they say, from the lips of the Prince of the Apostles by Clement himself concerning the revelations made known to Peter by the Lord between His resurrection and ascension. Now this book begins from the creation of the world and ends in the consummation of time; and in it are read the precepts and counsels of salvation. He inserts prophecies, certain of which now clearly appear to have been completed, though some depend upon the future. Among other things, it is said that a watery city would be captured by the Christians along with one city of Egypt. The capture of Alexandria is also added, nor is Damascus omitted, which greatly tortured and is still torturing the servants of God. Besides, mention is made of two kings, one of whom, it is claimed, will come from the East, the other from the West, to Jerusalem in that year when Easter will be on the third of April. This book agrees in many things with the one of which we made

4. Oliver states that King David was considered the son of Prester John. As mentioned in the note cited, others considered him to be John's nephew. This presumably refers to Jenghiz Khan's conquest of the Shah of Khwaresm, who could properly be called King of Persia.

1. Jacques de Vitry gives the correct title as *Revelationes beati Petri apostoli a discipulo eius Clemente in uno volumine redactae.*

mention above. Very many letters written about the victory of King David support this prophecy, along with the story well-known among Christians and Saracens. We also see as a proof of this that the Christian captives of this king were freed by messengers of King David in Baghdad; these had been taken in the siege of Damietta, and the King of Babylon had sent them to the Caliph as a gift.

Chapter 57

On July 17th, the Christian army gathered at Fareskur, a casale three miles distant from Damietta,[1] and being suitably drawn up in ranks of horsemen and troops of foot soldiers, they went forward quickly. Indeed estimators of the army enumerated twelve hundred men armed in military fashion, provided with the cavalry equipment necessary to accomplish such an undertaking, not counting the Turcopoles[2] and numerous other horsemen. We could not find out the exact count of armed foot soldiers because of their great number; the Saracens compared them to locusts because they occupied a great amount of land. We believe that four thousand archers assembled, almost twenty-five hundred of whom were mercenaries. Among the six hundred and thirty larger and smaller ships we clearly counted three hundred casques with eighteen armed galleys, and besides, there were scalanders, tartans,[3] barbots, corsairs, and barks carrying cargoes with provisions. The number of the enemy was declared by fugitives to have been about seven thousand horsemen. The arrangement of the battle line was as follows:

The river on the right, covered over with ships, afforded protection in the manner of a wall; on the left side, the foot soldiers served as a breastwork, going forward in line and in a procession, as it were, in close formation. The lines of horsemen were stretched out diagonally from the river to the

1. South of Damietta.
2. Natives of mixed origin who fought on horseback in native fashion. They were usually light cavalry or mounted archers, and are found in all the eastern armies from Byzantium to Cairo.
3. A small one-masted vessel with a large lateen sail and a foresail.

ranks of the foot soldiers, giving them support and receiving it from them. The lancers stayed constantly with the archers, sustaining the attack of the enemy with lances close-packed and leveled, if at any time they presumed to rush into close combat. Thus in the danger of horses and horsemen it was provided by prudent counsel that the pack animals should not be wounded. The common people, unarmed, proceeded in safety with their bundles at the bank of the river, clerics, foot soldiers, and women carried water to those farther off; those who were more experienced against the snares of the deceitful, cautiously sustained the attacks of the enemy in the fore and rear guard. By public edict severe precaution was taken that no one should presume to go ahead of the foremost ranks or to fall behind the rear line or to break into the line in any wise. The scouts of the enemy regarding our forces from both sides of the river and marveling at the order of our military discipline, tried in vain to inflict losses; but such a great multitude of archers resisted them that we learned that on that day none of our men had been captured and none of our men had been wounded, who had stayed constantly with the four-sided battle line. The Legate distributed wages with a generous hand to the knights and their attendants, he armed ships, sparing neither his body nor his possessions to accomplish the work, exhibiting all the diligence he could; in company with him King John of Jerusalem and the Duke of Bavaria, the archbishops and bishops, and the masters of the Houses toiled and labored at the undertaking.

Chapter 58

On July 19th the king of Egypt sent a stronger and greater proof of the might which he then had—four thousand horsemen, it seemed, who encircling the people of God timidly enough from without, at a distance, attacked the outermost lines of foot soldiers with arrows. Our men valiantly resisted them, not breaking their own lines in the least on account of this. On the following day, they besieged us more fiercely and compelled our men to use up quite a few arrows. In these two days the few Christians slightly wounded, and the very few dead, took away from the enemy the hope of winning a victory. Returning to their lord on the third day, they opened a peaceful way for us through Saramsah,[1] burning their casalia before us. Nevertheless we found plenty of grain and barley and vegetables, even straw, and the fruits of gardens; the inhabitants with their women and children fled altogether before the face of the power of God.

Chapter 59

On the vigil of Saint James [July 24] we pitched camp on a triangular head of an island where the Nile divides in two parts, and separates the former camp of the Sultan from ours, and where he had made a delay after the capture of Damietta. In this spot the river of Tanis, withdrawing from the bed which goes to Damietta, forms with it an island. This island, extending twelve miles in length, contains many casalia located above the waters. Among those on the farther shore better known than the others and more wealthy, are Symon and Saramsah, in which there were the magnificent palaces of the king. This island has obtained a name, and is called the land of Damietta; the one which is across the river is called the land of Tanis, but the wider one which is found across the river of Damietta is called Mahalech. Beyond the river of Tanis, less than one day's journey to the east, begins the solitude of the desert, in which, however, water is found at fixed watering places, sufficient for men and animals if it is increased by digging. Now it ends at Darum and Gaza.[1] Babylon, being located in the south, causes the land of Egypt to be called Babylonia. The plan of this city, divided into three parts, forms a triangle. The city of Babylon itself, built upon the Nile, is extensive in its length and width, having narrow streets and dwellings crowded together because of the great number of people. In it there are very many

1. Saramsah, a casale near the Nile, where the Sultan had a palace, described in the next chapter.

1. Darum and Gaza are on the southwestern coast of Palestine and marked the border between Palestine and Egypt.

churches of the Christians, and a numerous multitude of these same people serve the prince of the land under tribute. In it are set down the wares of traders coming from Lee-mannia,[2] Ethiopia, Libya, Persia, and other regions. From the side opposite Damietta at a distance of almost a mile, Cairo spreads out in buildings and spacious streets; it has magnificent mansions, in which the barons of the land and the nobler citizens stay. This city does not descend entirely to the river as does Babylon, but a space planted with rush-like roots is found between. At a distance a rather high watchtower, the royal fort, stands out, plain to see, and well protected by great towers. The great buildings are arranged in a threefold way after the manner of a triangle. Now from both sides of the fort the wall comes down, enclosing Cairo and Babylon, but a sandy stretch lies between these three buildings, in which a numerous army can remain.

Chapter 60

Between Cairo and Babylon they point out the Church of Blessed Mary where she is said to have made a pause with the Child Jesus, when she fled into Egypt and the idols of Egypt fell. Cairo is a three days' journey distant from Damietta. From Cairo to the garden of balsam, there is a distance of a mile; this garden, which has sandy soil, is enclosed by a wall. There is a fountain in the middle and from it is derived a tale of the ancient people which is spread abroad by a famous story, that the glorious Virgin drew it forth by her prayer, and washed the clothing of the Infant Savior in it. Now this garden is cultivated in the manner of vineyards. A trunk of this garden has the thickness of a plant; its branches shoot out from the trunk to the height of one cubit in the manner of a willow, and its bark is knotty and lined, and of a whitish color. Its wood is called sirobalsam, its seed, carpobalsam, its sparse and pointed leaf, like the leaf of the licorice, is called filobalsam, and also opobalsam in whose branches the farm-ers make cuts in certain parts of the bark where the balsam

2. According to Hoogeweg, this name is found nowhere else. Oliver seems to apply it to that part of Egypt which lay directly north of Ethiopia. (*See* Chapters 61 and 62.)

is drawn forth, so that the liquid, collecting by degrees, may run out through them. In autumn the balsam is collected in this way: A branch is twisted and scratched with a nail; through this small opening a drop is caught and kept in dishes; next it is melted for twenty days in the sun, and afterwards is skimmed off at the fire; the fluid is poured off into bottles, for of the original substance, very little unmixed balsam remains after the purification. But the sellers and resellers usually mix in pine resin or turpentine and deceive the buyers, and therefore it is rarely found pure at the hands of venders. The Sultan usually distributed it in bottles among the princes of the earth as a great gift. The master of this garden is a Christian, having Christian and Saracen servants under him.

Chapter 61

Below Cairo an island extends for a stretch of three miles in length and width, where the Nile divides its waters into two parts, touching the bank of Damietta on one side, and of Rosetta on the other. Rosetta was a great city, now in ruins, between Alexandria and Damietta, but much closer to Alexandria, and two days away from Cairo. At Rosetta and above it, the river is wider, the water deeper, the harbor calmer than at Damietta; for it receives heavily laden ships, and it is possible to place a large army on the aforesaid island. When we were at its head in the siege of Damietta, the Sultan wished to take the river from us; having tried often but in vain to cause its waters to flow into a channel; after great expense he left its course to nature. From Babylon on the upper side to Leemannia, the culture of the land is hedged in by both sides of the river, having vast solitudes on both sides. Leemannia abounds in a variety of spices which she sends out and which various traders of the kingdom carry away.

Chapter 62

Beyond Leemannia, Ethiopia holds very broad lands, and has an innumerable Christian population partly under Christian kings and partly under the rule of the Saracens. Here are the Nubians who are joined in the Sacrament of the Altar, and in other Jacobite divine offices,[1] with this exception: The Nubians are the only ones who imprint upon their little ones with heated iron a threefold character of the Cross on the forehead near the eyes on both sides. Nevertheless they do baptize. The former and the latter have the Chaldean writing; they use leavened bread for the Holy Eucharist; they make the sign of the Cross with one finger; they say that two natures are united in the one nature of Christ, perhaps using equivocally the name of nature, so that in the second place they take "nature" for "person."[2]

Chapter 63

The Georgians[1] and the Greeks agree in everything pertaining to divine services, but the Georgians have their own writing. While we were carefully examining their books on the mountain of Saint Simeon on the Pillar, where they have their own church, we learned through an interpreter that they have the same order of Gospels that the Latins have, and the canons of the Gospels on arcuated columns as we do. The order of the Epistles of Saint Paul is exactly the same with them as it is with us; they put the Epistle of Saint Paul to the Romans before all the others.

1. Jacobite is the usual name for the native Monophysite Christians (*see* n. 2, below) of Syria and Mesopotamia, named after James (Jacobus) el-Baradai by whom they were organized in the 6th century. They admit only the first three oecumenical councils, and claim that consecration in the liturgy is performed by the epiclesis—a prayer to send down the Holy Spirit on the bread and wine at Mass.

2. Monophysitism is the name given to the heresy that there is only one nature in Christ, His humanity being entirely absorbed in His divinity, and His body not of one substance with ours. It was an extreme reaction from Nestorianism, which stated that in Christ there were two persons joined together. Monophysitism was brought into wide discussion by Eutyches (448), but its chief defender was Dioscorus, Patriarch of Alexandria. It was officially condemned by the Council of Chalcedon (451) but never died out.

1. The Georgians formed an independent unit of the Orthodox Eastern Church. They were established in the 4th century, and entered into schism in the 13th.

Chapter 64

The Maronites[1] have their patriarchate on the side of Mount Lebanon. These received the plan of their ecclesiastical rites from Pope Innocent in the last Lateran Council, and they observe it insofar as their writing allows, which is Chaldean, or near-Chaldean. To these people on the side of the same mountain are joined the Neophorites[2] who keep their law concealed. They do not explain it to their sons and grandsons until the thirtieth year of their age. It is an evil law that desires to be kept secret and not to appear in the light. When we wished to know, as we were passing through that section, why they never revealed their law to their wives or daughters or sisters except at this age, one of the older men answered that women were made by the devil. And we responded, "When you embrace women of this kind, do you therefore embrace the devil?" Whereupon he withdrew from us confused. Certainly the Christians are sorry that they have such neighbors.

Chapter 65

The Armenians[1] have their own writing. In the field their priests set aside the grain from which they wish to make

1. A nation and church of Arabic-speaking Syrians who live chiefly in the Lebanon. Their name comes from St. Maron, a Syrian abbot who died in 433. They seem to have professed a heresy known as Monothelitism from the 7th century till 1182. Their union with Rome at that time is one of the few lasting results of the crusades.
2. Possibly the Neophorites are the same as the Druzes, a people of Asiatic Turkey and of Syria between Damascus to the east and Saida to the south. Their origin is full of fables, but they probably came from an Egyptian Mohammedan sect founded by the Caliph of Egypt, Hakim Biamrillah (996-1020), who founded a new sect of Ismalian Shiites. The Druzes now number about 200,000, and proved very bad neighbors to the Maronites in the 19th century.

1. The Armenian church dates back to at least the 3rd century and the work of St. Gregory the Illuminator. The Synod of Dovin in 527 adopted Monophysitism. Since that time the Armenian church has been the most national and the most isolated in Christendom. Reunion with Rome was proclaimed in 1198, but was never fully attained and failed completely in 1375. The rite still reveals much Latin influence.

unleavened hosts; they thresh it separately from the common crop; they grind it separately and on the day when they
wish to consecrate the Body of the Lord, with the singing of
psalms before the altar they prepare the flour and sprinkle
it with water for the Paschal bread, which is in the shape of
the Latins. They celebrate with great devotion. However,
they are very much to blame in this, that they do not celebrate the Nativity of the Lord with us;[2] they plough and sow
on that day while their women spin and card wool. They call
the day of the Epiphany "baptisterium"; on this solemnity
they assemble with a great crowd of people. They celebrate
the Nativity of the Lord with the Epiphany, saying that the
Lord was born on the same day as that on which He was
baptized after a few years had elapsed. They say that they are
subject to Roman laws and they have a catholicos as primate
whom they obey in all things.

Chapter 66

Stopping at Antioch, we carefully examine the Nestorians,[1]
who have their church there, and who say that they believe
that two natures are united in the person of Christ. They
confess that the Blessed Virgin is the mother of God and of
man, and that she bore both God and man, which Nestorius
denied. But whether they believe in their hearts as they
confess in their lips, God knows.

Chapter 67

The Syrians have the Greek writing, chant, and ritual sac-
rifice, but the Arabic language in common with the Saracens
in the deeds and letters which they draw up.

2. The Armenians are the only sect in the world who keep Christmas and
Epiphany (January 6) as one feast.

1. Nestorius, Bishop of Constantinople, who died *ca.* 451, stated that in
Christ two persons were joined together, namely, God the Son and the man
Jesus, Who alone was born of the Blessed Mother, and Who alone died on
the Cross. Nestorius' teachings were anathematized by the Council of
Ephesus (431), and his followers fled to Persia. They once formed a mighty,
but now small, Nestorian church.

Chapter 68

The Jacobites for the most part throughout Egypt are circumcised, but those who remain among the Medes and Persians are content with baptism.[1]

Chapter 69

The Russi have their own language, but in divine services they are found to be like the Greeks in everything. These different kinds of Christians are mingled with the Saracens throughout all Asia, and so that perfidious nation cannot excuse herself on the ground of ignorance.

Chapter 70

We have made this long digression not without reason, so that the location of Egypt and the course of the river as well as the variety of Christian inhabitants who are in Asia may appear more clearly to the faithful. Now, as we return to the order of our history, let us sprinkle this book with tears, weeping and grieving for the loss and disgrace of Christianity.

An advance to the great and famous casale of Saramsah, of which we made mention above, was of advantage to the army of Christ. Therefore, after the capture of Damietta, the Sultan, prudently looking out for what could happen in the future, destroyed the casale as well as his beautiful palace located on the Nile. Beyond that spot the river curves and turns back and a certain little stream, coming from the island of Mahalech, flows into it; taking on depth from the waters which increase as they spread out, it is able to bear galleys and other vessels of moderate size. When our leaders saw it, they scorned it and passed it by, hastening to the head of the island. The people also, in hopes of plunder, because it was

---

1. The Egyptian Monophysites are not Jacobites, but Copts. Oliver here uses an incorrect nomenclature for them.

falsely announced to them that the Sultan was preparing for flight, hurried eagerly like birds to a snare, and fishes to a net. But when the King of Babylon was informed that Saramsah had been abandoned from the rear, he united foot soldiers and horsemen from his own kingdom, from Cairo and Alexandria particularly, in an attack on those who were arriving. Whereupon, our captives, considering the fact that Cairo had been evacuated by its inhabitants, formed a plan to seize the towers at our arrival, and to open them to those who were approaching. But a divine Providence which mercifully "heard the groans of them that were in fetters,"[1] and the labors and sorrows of those who were in bondage, released them through our distress.

Chapter 71

While this was taking place in Egypt, Seraphus, King of Edessa,[1] the city of the Medes, with Cordin, Lord of Damascus, and the leaders of Hamah[2] and Homs[3] with a great multitude of horsemen, gathered from all regions of the east, and assembled at Homs. As a result great fear struck the people of Antioch and Acre, and other cities on the coast whose warriors were absent since they had set out on an expedition. Those in Safita, in the country of Tripoli, were especially concerned about this assemblage.

Long and earnestly did the forenamed princes deliberate whether they should come to the aid of Egypt themselves, or whether they should divide the army of the Christians by besieging some one of their fortresses. The power of King David influenced them, since as victor over the king of the Persians in the lands of the Persians and in those of Baghdad, he was acting powerfully, and on account of him they were afraid to go far from their own lands. They also reflected that

1. Psalms 101:21.

1. He was called King of Aleppo previously.
2. The classical Epiphania, on the Orontes in Syria. It belonged to an Ayyubid house, descended from Taki ed din, a nephew of Saladin.
3. In Syria, about 90 miles north-northeast of Damascus.

the castles of the Hospitallers or the Templars could not easily be captured in a short time. Finally the counsel of those who urged advance into Egypt prevailed, especially because their brother frequently sent messengers on courier camels begging them to come. He added that the Christians had taken up their position in such a place that they could not leave it without danger, or that if they could not prevail against them when they came, they would at least arrange peace with them. The Queen of Cyprus wrote to the Legate, and the brothers of the Hospital and of the Temple wrote to their masters about these troops and their plan, urging them not to retreat from Damietta; or, if they had gone out, to look out for themselves in safe places. But now just when the sins of us all needed it, sane counsel was far removed from our leaders; like Julius Caesar,[4] repeatedly forewarned, and like Alexander the Macedonian,[5] warned in the silence of the night, they neglected to employ precautions against physical danger. The Lord Himself spoke through Moses to the sons of Israel: "Go not up nor fight, for I am not with you, lest you fall before your enemies."[6] They went up, none the less, and they fell conquered. But King John, reflecting more deeply on the matter, wisely showed that the proposal so often proffered by the enemy ought to be accepted, rather than that the people of the faithful, being led forth on a longer march, should be exposed to chance accidents. But the Supreme Pontiff forbade any agreement without a special degree of the Roman Church; the Emperor, through letters sealed with gold, would not permit peace or a treaty to be arranged with the Saracens.[7]

4. See Suetonius, De Vita Caesarum, I, 83.
5. See Curtius Rufus, Historiae Alexandri Magni, X, 4.
6. Numbers 14:42.
7. Pelagius had been instructed to communicate any proposed terms to the Pope. When Honorius learned the terms of Al-Kamil, he replied that he regretted the loss of life, the labor, and the expense entailed in refusing them, but that Frederick's recent assurance that he woul sail to the East made him decide against accepting them. Honorius was influenced also by the reports concerning "Prester John" and "King David" that were prevalent, reports really based on the exploits of Jenghiz Khan and his Tartars. Frederick also, in several letters, forbade that Damietta be exchanged for Jerusalem.

Chapter 72

Meanwhile we strengthened our fort by a deep ditch; on the other hand our adversaries made a wall of earth and high bulwarks on the opposite banks of both rivers, setting up on them machines, petraries, and ballistae with a lathe, causing serious injury to the men and to the animals who were taken out to drink. The strength of our adversaries increased daily; our gathering, being depleted, proved unfaithful. As the time for passage drew near, timidity increased among those who, going away openly or deceitfully, deserted us in the camp. Many ships also, that went to Damietta to bring food, could not return. For on the 18th day of August four of our galleys were captured or sunk in the river; this gave added courage to the enemy. For the Sultan had sunk some of his galleys all through the river, of which we made mention above, below our camp through the island of Mahalech at the bank of the river, without our knowledge; this cut off passage for our men, so that they could go neither up nor down. Besides, since a multitude of armed men had wisely been stationed there, a continual guard night and day watched both banks as far as Damietta, so that our people could neither send nor receive messengers.

Chapter 73

From the day when we lost the river our men frequently assembled to consult together, and to ponder what would be more expedient: to wait in camp for the galleys promised by the emperor, or to go out, no matter what the loss, because of our dwindlinge supply of food. The greater number counseled going out, which was more dangerous because of the arrival of the enemy and the decided hindrance of the waters. But a certain one of the lesser members,[1] who saw and heard these things and described them with a crude but truthful pen, proposed David as an example, who having choice among three things, any one of which was hard, chose

1. Oliver himself.

not a famine of seven years, nor to be conquered by an
enemy for three months, but what was the common wish of
the king and the poor people: a pestilence of three days.
Wherefore he answered, when he was consulted, as did the
weak and infirm whom there were not sufficient ships nor
animals to carry, that help should be awaited in a fortified
place, since the provisions, if they were carefully distributed,
could last even for twenty days. Nevertheless this plan was
not accepted, but a departure, and that by night, was more
favored. In this, the opinion of the Bishop of Passau and that
of the Bavarians prevailed.

Chapter 74

Therefore on August 26th in the first watch of the night,
when the tents were taken up, the first men, following the
judgment of their own will, and not that of reason, put fire
to the tents; then others also did it eagerly, as if they were
announcing their own flight, and inviting the Egyptians, who
had already surrendered their bodies to sleep, to follow us.
At the same time the Nile had received its full increase, and,
as its waters surged even higher than usual, it had flooded the
fields. The forenamed kings also came through the desert
above the river Tanis at Symon, where a bridge was built,
and stopped and encamped. It added greatly to our misfortune that the people were greatly intoxicated that day with
wine of which there was such an abundance that it culd not
be brought along; but being freely exposed, it had over-
whelmed the unwary, who remained sound asleep in the
camp or prostrate on the road. They were unwilling to be
roused, and in great part they left us, being either cut off or
captured. Others came into the overflow of the river in the
shadows of night, and struggling wretchedly in the deep
mire, stayed behind the others. Others, falling into the ships
and pressing them down too much with their weight, were
drowned. On the same night we lost camels and mules carrying burdens, including the silver vessels, clothing, and tents
of the rich, and what was more disastrous, the arrows of

defense. The Templars, bringing up the rear at their own great risk, stayed constantly together as a protection for those who went ahead, as they were prepared with weapons. But those who went ahead, going into different roads, wandered through the darkness of the night like sheep astray. The Egyptians were informed of our flight by the fire and smoke and promptly followed after us. They reached us even more quickly and inflicted on the Christians losses which we cannot describe. No less danger and injury was sustained by those who went down in a ship along the bank. The ship of the Legate, carrying a great number of the sick, as well as provisions, was extremely well fortified with armed men and archers, just as if it were a fort, and valiantly protected the galleys which naturally stayed close together; but hurrying too much, perhaps because of the force of the current, and being fatally separated from the land army, it could not supply food to us àt the proper time. Furthermore, one of our ships filled with German warriors got too far away from the Legate's ship and was surrounded on all sides by galleys of the enemy; while sinking one of them into the deep after a long defense, it caught fire and destroyed the combatants. A scalander of the Legate carrying many temporal goods, and one small galley of the Templars in which were fifty ballistae, besides other equipment of brave men, was seized and went out of our possession.

Why do I linger over the enumeration of the losses which that night caused us? "Let a darksome whirlwind seize upon that night, let it not be counted in the days of the year, nor numbered in the months. Let that night be solitary and not worthy of praise."[1] In the beginning of this night the King of Egypt, quickly sending messengers, had the sluices broken (which those people usually call "calig") through which there could be a passage for us. Their own night is memorable to the Egyptians, and to us also. When the banks had been burst to a great extent, the superabundance of water, following the declivity of the reservoirs through conduits, softened the earth, made dry by long drought, into sticky mud which

1. Job 3:6-7.

held tight the horses' hoofs; it made the open space of the fields quite impassable and greatly hindered horses and riders.

Chapter 75

Around the first hour of the following Friday [Aug. 27] there appeared the great and fearful cavalry of the Turks harassing us at the right; annoying galleys went up and down at the left; a phalanx of Negroes going on foot and using the marshy places for a camp pressed upon us savagely from the rear; and also a wedge-shaped formation of enemies, coming from the front, denied us rest. In this contingency King John made an attack on the Turks who were opposite him, and returned to his own battle line. The Templars, with the Hospitallers of Saint John who at that time were united with them, did not tolerate the insolence of the Ethiopians. As they massacred them they made them jump onto the bank like frogs, and even drove them back when they wished to approach the bank on our side. Thus about a thousand of the great multitude, swimming away or suffering wounds, perished. On account of this misfortune our opponents retreated a little. And since we were not permitted to go forward, the king ordered a few tents, which had stayed behind, to be taken up; nevertheless, through that whole day our adversaries stayed close to us, attacking us fiercely with their archers. We put our foot soldiers against them as a rampart and used them also, for they shot back the arrows directed against us. Our horsemen, laboring under the constant weight of their armor, served as a protection to the foot soldiers. On the following night, whether by the command of the Sultan or without his knowledge, the Egyptians broke open the floodgates and made the waters pour in upon the heads of those who were sleeping. Before daybreak, when darkness still covered the earth, the Ethiopian foot soldiers came who had escaped the grasp of the river, desiring to avenge their losses; they swarmed like locusts, and although for the greater part they were naked, they attacked our rear lines. You could see that our knights and their attendants were attempting flight in a closely packed throng; and the common people, being unarmed, displayed manifest timidity, but being blocked on all sides by the waters and the enemy, they had nowhere to flee. However, the Marshal of the Temple with his battle line which he was leading, raised his banner, turned upon those who were pursuing, and forced them to halt and retreat.

Chapter 76

At this juncture, distress which gave understanding persuaded the leaders of the multitude to send messengers for terms of peace. But Imbert,[1] a worker of great evil, took with him those whom he could get away, and went over to the enemy, explaining the whole of our distress to the Sultan. This Imbert usually took part in the secret councils of the Lord Legate, and was by far the worst traitor of that time. Nevertheless, the Sultan heard the messengers patiently, and, pending a confirmation, ordered his men to cease from disturbing us. And although his brother, and especially the Lord of Homs, who was extremely hostile to the name of Christian, tried to dissuade him from an agreement, saying that since the Franks were blocked on all sides by water, they could not escape, he himself, like a wise and mild man, desired an arrangement of peace more than the shedding of blood. Therefore, he held a secret council with his brothers and the great men of his kingdom. He proposed as an example the King of the Persians, who was exceedingly lifted up in mind because of many events, and shook off the yoke of subjection or servitude to the King of Babylon himself and other kings of Asia. King David conquered him on the battlefield, took away Persia, and destroyed its greatest and wealthiest cities. After this, the messengers of peace spoke on both sides, as is usually done in matters of this kind,

---

1. The identity of this traitor Imbert is not known. Oliver seems to be the only author who mentions him.

and protracted the business all through the Saturday and Sunday following, even until evening, settling upon nothing definite.

Chapter 77

On the very day of the Beheading of Saint John the Baptist [Aug. 29], at about the twelfth hour, our side, urged on by the lack of food and fodder, but especially by the great size of the waters, decided that it was more honorable to live happily or to die bravely in war, than to perish infamously in the flood. So when all the Franks had been roused to combat, battle lines were drawn up here and there looking upon each other fiercely and dreadfully. But the Turks realized that he who provokes an enemy is by his own fault bound by a yoke; they retreated a little upon receiving a command from their King, and the arrival of nightfall prevented a battle. Besides, while the treaty of peace was pending, a display of treachery was feared by wise men, if the common good were to be destroyed by a dangerous attack.

Chapter 78

And so on the 30th day of August, being forced into a lamentable peace by the perversity of circumstances, we surrendered to the Egyptians and Assyrians, that we might be filled with bread; and thus the flood of waters and the lack of food, not the bow or the sword, humbled us in the land of our enemies. An astonishing thing, an astounding thing, a thing to be handed down to the knowledge of the future: At one and the same time the just judgment of divinity appeared and the moderation of mercy shone clearly in opportune assistance. The enormity of our evil deeds and the vast number of our crimes were compelling the vengeance of divine decision, but the natural Fount of Goodness, Whose property it is always to have mercy and to spare, mitigated the sentence of just severity. For this did we fall into danger, that by the mediation of mercy, a miracle might shine forth. "God will not have His creature to perish, and recalling, intends that he that is cast off should not altogether perish."[1] The angel of great counsel, speaking for man, as one among thousands appealed for us, announcing the justice of man;[2] for although we may be sinners, nevertheless, carrying His Cross we have left homes or parents or wives or brothers or sisters or sons or fields for the sake of Him Who shows anger placidly, Who judges calmly, Who chastises lovingly, having the blows of a father, but the heart of a mother.

Chapter 79

And so when the conditions had been laid down according to the decisions of the Sultan, the documents of the contracts were completed by both sides, oaths were sworn, and hostages were named. The Sultan, therefore, placing his right hand on a paper which he had signed, swore in this way: "I, Kamil, King of Babylon, from a pure heart and a good will, and without interruption, do swear by the Lord, by the Lord, by the Lord and my law, that I will in good faith observe all the things that this written paper contains which is placed under my hand; if I shall not do this, may I be separated from future judgment and the society of Mohammed, and may I acknowledge the Father, the Son, and the Holy Ghost." In this manner swore Seraphus and Coradin, and their more eminent emirs. Behold under how many mistakes and contradictions is that blind nation laboring; three times they name God, but not knowing the mystery of the Trinity, they are unwilling to distinguish the name of the Father, of the Son, and of the Holy Ghost, to the increase of their own damnation. If they swear in bad faith or with any interruption of the form of the ritual, they say that they are not under obligation. Now this writing contained an agreement of this

1. II Kings 14:14.
2. *See* Job 33:23. The Latin text as given by Hoogeweg seems in need of a slight emendation. Oliver is clearly quoting the Latin text of Job which has *unus de millibus* (one among thousands). By an easily understandable slip of the pen Oliver's text now has *unum de similibus*, which does not make very clear sense.

kind: that they would restore the True Cross,[1] along with all captives taken any time at all in the kingdom of Babylon, or all Christians held in the power of Coradin; and that when they had received Damietta with all its belongings, they would send us all away free, as well as all our movable goods, and would faithfully keep a truce of eight years. Our leaders swore that they would free all Saracen captives, whom they were holding in the two kingdoms of Egypt and Jerusalem; that they would restore Damietta and would observe the treaty, unless our crowned King who was coming should wish to break it. Besides, twenty-four hostages were given, whom the Sultan chose: the Legate, the King of Jerusalem, the Duke of Bavaria, and three masters of Houses, along with eighteen others. On the other hand, the son of the Sultan, heir of the kingdom, and one of his brothers of whom there are many, and sons of nobles were given to us until our return to Turo[2] and the port of Damietta.

Chapter 80

Let all posterity know that in view of the critical point of our necessity, we made an excellent bargain, when the Wood of our redemption was restored to us in exchange for one city which Christianity could not hold for long, since grain or wheat is spoiled there in less than a year and the master of Egypt himself can scarcely keep it peopled; and when so many thousands of captives, in whose number we counted ourselves, from the greatest to the least, were restored to their own freedom. When the Emperor Heraclius entered Persia, he captured it with difficulty after five successive years; and having defeated Chosroes, he carried the Cross of the Lord in triumph and brought the patriarch Zachary back to Jerusalem with his captive people. The Sultan had been

1. The earliest reference to the existence of the True Cross was made by St. Cyril of Jerusalem in 347. The Empress Helena is said to have divided the Cross into three parts, sending one to the church of Jerusalem. It was this section that the Mohammedans had taken.
2. Situated near Damietta.

keeping as captive the Patriarch of Alexandria,[1] a man of great piety and perfection of morals; he sent him back to us as we were going up the Nile, released from his chains and free from the squalor of prison. The enemies of the Cross declare that they were deceived in this agreement, saying that they had regained their own city of Damietta, that they had destroyed Jerusalem, and other fortresses of this illustrious kingdom, but that the Christians had erected one impregnable fort in Palestine itself, very dangerous to them and without their consent.[2] Besides, if we had been completely destroyed, or imprisoned after losing all our possessions, and if Damietta had been lost without any recompense, the rest of the land which the worshipers of Christ hold would have wavered on the edge of certain danger. For those who had remained to guard Damietta, when they heard our adverse circumstances, left the city and fled, for the most part. Not only did they flee, but also those who had but recently arrived heard the unfavorable report and returned.[3] The Count of Malta[4] reached Damietta around the end of August with forty galleys. Pirates despoiled the Hospitallers of Saint John and the Templars of their goods, killed one noble knight and religious brother of the Temple who was defending what had been entrusted to him, and fatally wounded another brother, a Teutonic knight.

Chapter 81

Before the restoration of Damietta the Sultan began to carry out what he had promised. For he commanded that the Bishop-elect of Beauvais and certain other captives be released from chains and brought to their own camp. The Master of the army of the Temple and the Master of

---

1. Since 1219 this see had been occupied by Athanasius of Clermont in Auvergne.
2. Château-Pélerin.
3. The surrender of the city followed on September 8.
4. Henry Pescatore, Count of Malta, had been sent by Emperor Frederick as admiral of his fleet.

the Teutonic House[1] were sent by the leaders to surrender the city in accordance with the pledge and assurance of their oath. This was done without great difficulty. For
among the new pilgrims who were arriving, there was not to
be found a man powerful, vigorous, and constant enough to
be either willing or able to hold it after the forementioned
happenings.

Chapter 82

"The beast has gone into his covert, and abides in his den."[1]
If it is asked why Damietta returned so quickly to the unbelievers, the reason is clear: It was luxury-loving, it was
ambitious, it was mutinous; besides, it was exceedingly ungrateful to God and to men. For to pass over other things,
when that city had been given to us from on high by Heaven
in the distribution of the riches that were found in her, not
an old woman nor a boy of ten years and over was excluded;
to Christ alone, the bestower of the goods, was a share denied, not even a tenth being paid to Him. Formerly Roman
pagans dedicated a golden vessel to Apollo under the form
of tithes; the sons of Israel according to custom assigned to
the Lord His share of the spoils of the enemy; the sons of
Israel said to Moses when they had conquered the Madia-
nites, "We offer as gifts to the Lord what gold we could find
in the booty, in garters, rings, tablets, bracelets, and chains."[2]
   In the distribution of towers and dwellings most praise was
deservedly given to that obedient and energetic nation,[3]
who from the beginning attacked Damietta with great courage, and considered no position either humble or lowly; by
the fleet of ships which it brought, the camp of the faithful
was supplied with food and weapons, the tower of the river
was captured, the crossing to the opposite bank was organized, the upper and lower bridges were built, the watch-

1. The Master of the Teutonic Knights at this time was the famous Herman von Salza, the ultimate councilor of Frederick II.
   1. Job 37:8.
   2. Numbers 31:50.
   3. The Frisians.

tower of Turo was constructed, the walls of the rampart were fortified. It has consolation in the face of such ingratitude since "God will render the inestimable reward" of His slaves "and will conduct them in a wonderful way."[4]

Chapter 83

O lover of men, King of glory, Savior of the world, Who hast holy knowledge and omnipotence above all power, Who dost reprove some and dost console others, Thou didst humble our pride by taking away Damietta from the ungrateful and by mercifully preserving Armenia and Antioch against the efforts of wicked men. For those who were in the fortress inflicted great disaster upon Christianity, but those who were then in the valley added irreverence to wickedness; as they presumptuously gathered in defiance of Thy goodness, from one side Thy justice appeared plainly, and from another the mercy of Thy customary goodness clearly shone on those who were willing to open their eyes.

Chapter 84

Rupen, formerly Lord of Antioch, was of very noble stock, but because of a lack of discretion he was unsuitable for the management of great things; with the help of Guérin, Master of the Hospital of Saint John,[1] and of those whom he could persuade, he seized Tarsus, attacking the Armenians because of a desire for kingdom. This did not escape the Turcomans of Iconium. They were encouraged by the discord of the Christians, and attacked Armenia with troops. But as the leaders of that kingdom, in making their complaint, affirm

---

4. Wisdom 10:17.

---

1. Guérin of Montagu, a Frenchman from the province of Auvergne, brother of Eustorgius, Archbishop of Nicosia and Peter, Master of the Temple. He was acting as Marshal of the Hospitallers when he was promoted to be Grand Master in 1208. He distinguished himself at the siege of Damietta. He had assisted at the coronation of John of Brienne in 1210, and had attended the Parliament of Acre in 1217. He died in 1228, and was succeeded by Bernard of Texis.

and state on peril of their lives, the army of Christians in that region at that time was reduced to about twenty thousand after they counted those who had been killed or captured by the Saracens, and also after many had fled because of the loss of their goods.

Chapter 85

Therefore in addition to all Thy praise, insofar as I am able and as Thou wilt permit, I shall continue by adding the following things.

Chapter 86

In the year of grace 1222 in the month of May it happened that there was a great earthquake on Cyprus, in Limasol, Nicosia, and other places of that island, especially in Paphos, to such a degree that the city was completely destroyed along with the fort; human beings of both sexes who were there at the time of the earthquake were completely lost; the harbor was dried up, where afterwards waters or fountains burst forth.

Chapter 87

In the month of June in that same year Coradin assembled a numerous army from Arabia, Palestine, Idumea, and Syria —ten thousand horsemen, and fifteen thousand foot soldiers —against Guy of Gibelet who, like a vain and wicked man, did not wish to take part in the general truce, nor to return the captive Saracens whom he held. Although he was well enough fortified by the difficult nature of the region and by the help of Christians, nevertheless he submitted to a truce with Coradin that was injurious to him and shameful to the Christian name.[1]

1. Border warfare was rather usual in the north of the kingdom, even after the peace had been made. On this occasion, Guy simply refused to recognize the truce, and was compelled by Al-Moadden to a separate truce.

Chapter 88

In the month of June in the same year, the boy Philip, son of Bohemond, Prince of Antioch, became a knight in Armenia; he married the daughter of Leo, formerly King of Armenia, and was solemnly crowned with her as King of that kingdom. And when the nuptials were being celebrated, and the Armenians were joyfully assembled for the great affair, Turks from Iconium savagely attacked that land with a great multitude, massacring whomever they could find and taking away much plunder with them. At the same time Bohemond, Prince of Antioch and Count of Tripoli, was present. Although he had only a few Latins with him at the time, since he had not foreseen this mishap, nevertheless, with his son the king he promptly and vigorously pursued the enemy over long, hard roads. Although many of his number were killed, like a vigorous man, and one skilled in arms, he drove them out beyond the boundaries of Armenia. After this, the Armenians recovered a certain well fortified camp, Siblia[1] by name, located at the boundaries of Armenia and Turkey, which the Sultan of Iconium had taken away from them along with other fortresses after the death of Leo.

Chapter 89

Meanwhile Frederick, Emperor of the Romans and King of Sicily, sent four galleys to Acre, summoning the King, the Patriarch, and the Master of the Hospital of Saint John. They crossed in the month of September, hastening to the Council of Verona, which had been proclaimed by the Supreme Pontiff and the Emperor for the feast of Saint Martin [Nov. 11]. At the same time, along with the forementioned princes, came Lord Pelagius, Bishop of Albano, a Legate of the Apostolic See. The Master of the Temple, with the army of the same House, remained in the land of promise for the protec-

---

1. Identified as Sandakli in Phrygia by Röhricht.

tion of Christianity, according to the common advice of the barons, after sending discreet and honorable messengers to the Council.

Appendix: Concluding Section of the Darmstadt Manuscript[1]

When this had been so accomplished, our pilgrims grew sluggish through idleness and riotous living, and, being eager for earthly gain, they provoked the wrath of the Almighty against themselves. When He saw that we were ungrateful for the blessings we had received He judged us unworthy to receive more. Truly, since neither power nor triumph is long-lived without God on account of our sins, which in their different uncleannesses had offended the Author of our salvation, certain sons of Belial, under a false pledge of Christian faith, deceitfully suggested to us that we set out against the Sultan with all the force of our army which had been stationed in nearby forts with a multitude of pagans as great as the sands of the sea which cannot be numbered. But, hoping that the affair would be accomplished by the Lord our God, in accordance with the common advice of the pilgrims, we set out against the enemies of the faith, unwisely leaving Damietta without defense. When the Sultan, after three days, saw the flight of the pilgrims, he pretended flight on his own part, and deceitfully left his camp to be plundered by us. With the whole strength of Egypt he hurried swiftly to Damietta by another road, and established his camp in a narrow spot below the city and us, so that we could have neither retreat nor intercourse with it. Behold how sudden a change of the right hand of the Most High! Then, with God favorable to us, we reigned mightily in the land of Egypt; now, with Him against us, we drift wretchedly between Scylla and Charybdis, between hunger and thirst. For this is

1. In the Darmstadt manuscript of the present work, Chapter 53 is followed by this concluding section, which was probably written by another hand.

that day of which it is written: "That day is a day of wrath,"[2] etc. Sorrow and groaning and the moisture of tears do not permit me to describe our tribulations and distresses, and the particular dangers of death. But since nothing was left for us but a wretched death, we all with one voice cried out to heaven to Our Lord Jesus Christ humbly begging pardon. But He Who says in His kindness, "I desire not the death of the wicked but rather that he be converted and live,"[3] frequently, when He is angry, is mindful of His mercy and is also just and merciful. Since He now saw that we had been sufficiently purified by penance and a fountain of tears, He mitigated the cruelty of our enemies to such an extent that they sent messengers to us, who were wasting away with hunger, to treat of peace and concord with us, on these terms: That the Sultan might take back his city to be possessed in peace, and that he would give us safe conduct to it along with complete integrity of our persons and belongings by supplying adequate ships and provisions. But we knew that the delegation had been procured by God, since there was nothing else left for us but death or the everlasting disgrace of slavery; and we willingly embraced it, humbly returning deserved thanks to God. When these agreements had been firmly settled through hostages and oaths, the Sultan was moved by such compassion toward us that for many days he freely revived and refreshed our whole multitude. Finally when our affair had been disposed and settled, he procured ships and provisions for a just price, along with safe conduct. Who could doubt that such kindness, mildness, and mercy proceeded from God? Those whose parents, sons, and daughters, brothers and sisters we killed with various tortures, whose property scattered or whom we cast naked from their dwellings, refreshed us with their own food as we were dying of hunger, although we were in their dominion and power. And so with great sorrow and mourning we left the port of Damietta, and according to our different nations, we separated to our everlasting disgrace.

2. Sophonias, 1:15.
3. Ezechiel, 33:11.

3. Three Letters from the East: from the Chronicle of Roger of Wendover

Of the Condition of the Holy Land after the Capture of Damietta and Tannis, 1221

[About this time the master of the knights of the temple sent the following letter on the state of affairs in the Holy Land:]—"To our reverend brother in Christ N., by the grace of God, bishop of Elimenum, Peter de Montacute, master of the knights of the temple, greeting. How we have proceeded in the business of our Lord Jesus Christ since the capture of Damietta and the castle of Tannis, we by these present letters set forth to your holiness. Be it known to you then that, in the first passage after the aforesaid captures, such a number of pilgrims arrived at Damietta that, with the rest of the army which remained, they were sufficient to garrison Damietta and to defend the camp. Our lord the legate and the clergy, desirous to advance the cause of the army of Christ, often and earnestly exhorted the people to make an attack on the infidels, but the nobles of the army, as well those of the transmarine provinces as those on our side of the water, thinking that the army was not sufficient for the defence of the aforesaid cities and castles, and at the same time to proceed further for the advantage of Christianity, would not consent to this plan; for the sultan of Babylon, with an innumerable host of infidels, had pitched his camp near Damietta, and on each arm of the river had built bridges to obstruct the progress of the Christians, and was there waiting with such an immense army that the crusaders, by proceeding further would incur the greatest danger. Nevertheless we fortified the said city and camp and the coast round with trenches in all directions, expecting to be consoled by the Lord with the assistance of those who were coming to help us; the Saracens, however, seeing our deficiency, armed all their galleys and sent them to sea in the month of September, and these caused great loss amongst the Christians who were coming to the assistance of the Holy Land. In our army there was such a great deficiency of money that we could not maintain our ships for any length of time. Therefore, knowing that great loss would be incurred by the Christian army by means of these said galleys of the Saracens, we immediately armed our galleys, galliots, and other vessels to oppose them. Be it also known to you that Coradin the sultan of Damascus assembled an immense army of Saracens, and, finding that the cities of Acre and Tyre were not sufficiently supplied with knights and soldiers to oppose him, continually did serious injury to those places both secretly and openly; besides this he often came and pitched his camp before our camp which is called the Pilgrims', doing us all kinds of injury; he also besieged and reduced the castle of Caesarea in Palestine, although numbers of Pilgrims were staying in Acre. I have also to inform you that Seraph, a son of Saphadin, and brother of the sultans of Babylon and Damascus, is with a powerful army fighting against the Saracens in the eastern parts, and has prevailed much against the more powerful of his enemies, although not against all, for, by God's favour, he will not be able easily to conquer all of them; for if he could bring that war to a conclusion, the county of Antioch or Tripoli, Acre or Egypt, whichever of them he might turn his attention to, would be in the greatest danger, and if he were to lay siege to any one of our castles, we should in no wise be able to drive him away; this said dissension amongst the pagans however gives us pleasure and comfort. Moreover we have long expected the arrival of the emperor and other nobles by whom we hope to be relieved, and on their arrival we hope to bring this business, which has commenced by the hands of many, to a happy termination; but if we are deceived in our hope of this assistance in the ensuing summer, which I hope will not happen, both countries, namely Syria and Egypt, and that which we have lately gained possession of as well as that which we have held for a long time, will be placed in a doubtful position. Besides, we and the other people on our side of the water are oppressed by so many and great expenses in carrying on this crusade, that we shall be unable to meet our necessary expenses, unless by the divine mercy we shortly receive assistance from our fellow Christians. Given at Acre the 20th of September."

Of the Loss of Damietta, 1222

"To his worshipful lord and friend R. earl of Chester and Lincoln, his ever faithful P. de Albeney, health and sincere affection. I have to inform your excellency that on the day of the Assumption of the Virgin Mary we sailed from the port of Marseilles, and on the Monday before the Nativity of the same virgin we arrived before Damietta, and there we saw many ships leaving the town, and I spoke with a certain vessel, and made presents to the crew, on which they came to speak to us, and brought us very sad reports. These were that our people at Damietta and the nobles in that city, namely, the king of Jerusalem, the legate, the duke of Bavaria, the templars and hospitallers, with many others, amounting to about a thousand crusaders and five thousand other knights with forty thousand foot-soldiers, had all gone on an expedition towards Babylon, against the wish of the king of Jerusalem, as was said, having set out on the feast of St. Peter *ad vincula;* that they had been now absent on that expedition three weeks or more, and were about half way between Damietta and Babylon. The sultan of Babylon and his brother Coradin, then came with all the forces they could muster, and often attacked our people, and often lost some of their own men; and when our people wished to return to Damietta, the river became swollen, and for several days overflowed its banks, and our people were between two branches of the river; the Saracens then made a canal from one branch to the other in the rear of our army, whilst the river increased so in height, that our people were in water up to their legs and waists, to their great misery and suffering, and thus might have been either slain or taken prisoners if the sultan of Babylon wished it. In this condition our people agreed to a truce for eight years with the sultan, on the condition that they should give up Damietta and all the prisoners whom they held in captivity. For the due observance of this truce, the king of Jerusalem, the legate, the duke of Bavaria, and other influential people, remained as hostages; and the sultan had given twenty hostages for the due observance of the truce on his part. When we heard these reports we were much grieved, as all Christians must need be; we therefore thought it best, as we did not wish to be present at the surrender of Damietta, to make our way to Acre, where we arrived on the day after the Nativity of the Virgin Mary; on the day following Damietta was given up to the sultan, and he himself set free all the prisoners in it. I have also to inform you that his majesty the king of Jerusalem is about to go to your country; therefore I beg of you that you afford him assistance according to promises made towards the king and other nobles, for it is difficult to describe his great and admirable merits."

Another Letter about the Same Matters, 1222

"Brother P. de Montacute, humble master of the knights of the temple, to his well-beloved brother in Christ, A. Martel, holding the office of preceptor in England, greeting.— Although we have from time to time informed you of the prosperity which attended us in the affairs of Jesus Christ, we now by this present letter relate to you in the order they have happened the reverses which we, owing to our sins, have met with in the land of Egypt. The Christian army after the capture of Damietta having remained quietly at that place for a long time, the people of our side of the water, as well as those of the transmarine provinces, cast reproofs and reproaches on us on that account; and the duke of Bavaria having arrived, as lieutenant of the emperor, explained to the people that he had come for the purpose of attacking the enemies of the Christian faith. A council therefore was held by our lord the legate, the duke of Bavaria, the masters of the templars and hospitallers, and the Teutonic order, the earls, barons, and all the rest, at which it was unanimously agreed by all to make an advance. The illustrious king of Jerusalem also, having been sent for, came with his barons, and with a fleet of galleys and armed ships to Damietta, and found the army of the Christians lying in their camp outside the lines. After the feast of the apostles Peter and Paul, then his majesty the king and the legate, with the whole Christian army, proceeded in order both by land and water, and discovered the sultan with an innumerable host of the enemies of the cross, who however fled before them; and so they proceeded without loss till they arrived at the camp of the sultan; this was surrounded by the river which they were unable to cross; the Christian army therefore pitched its camp on the bank, and constructed bridges to cross over against the sultan, from whose camp we were separated by the river Tannis, which is a branch of the great river Nile. Whilst we made some stay there, great numbers left our army without leave, so that it was decreased by ten thousand men or more. In the meantime the sultan, by means of a trench constructed previously, when the Nile rose, sent galleys and galliots into the river to obstruct our ships, that no supplies might come from Damietta to us, we being then destitute of provisions; for·they could not reach us by land, as the Saracens prevented them. The road both by sea and land, by which necessary supplies could reach us, being thus blocked up, the army held council as to returning; but the brothers of the sultan, Seraph and Coradin, the sultans of Aleppo and Damascus, and other sultans, namely, of Camela, Haman, and Coilanbar, with many pagan kings, and a countless host of infidels, who had come to assist them, had cut off our retreat. Our army however departed by night by land and water, but lost all the provisions in the river, besides a great many men; for when the Nile overflowed, the sultan turned the water in different directions by means of hidden streams, canals, and rivulets, which had been made some time before to obstruct the retreat of the Christians. The army of Christ therefore, after losing amongst the marshes all its beasts of burden, stores, baggage, carriages, and almost all their necessaries, and being destitute of provisions, could neither advance nor retreat, nor had it any place of refuge, neither could it give battle to the sultan on account of his being surrounded by the river, and it was thus caught in the midst of the waters like a fish in a net. Being therefore in this strait, they, although unwillingly, agreed to give up to the sultan the city of Damietta, with all the prisoners which could be found in Tyre and Acre, in exchange for the true cross and the Christian prisoners in the kingdoms of Babylon and Damascus. We therefore, in company with other messengers deputed by the army in common, went to Damietta, and told the people of the city the terms which were imposed on us; which greatly displeased the bishop of Acre, the chancellor, and Henry count of Malta, whom we found there: for they wished to defend the city, which we should also have much approved of, if it could have been done with any advantage, for we had rather been consigned to perpetual imprisonment, than that the city should be given up by us to the infidels to the disgrace of Christianity; we therefore made a careful search throughout the city of all persons and effects, but found neither money nor people wherewith it could be defended. We therefore acquiesced in this agreement, and bound ourselves by oath and by giving hostages, and agreed to a confirmed truce for eight years. The sultan, till the arrangement was made, strictly abided by what he had promised, and supplied our famished army with loaves and flour for about fifteen days. Do you therefore, compassionating our sufferings, assist us as far as you are able. Farewell."

IV. The Emperor's Crusade, 1227-1229

1. The Crusade of Frederick II: From the Chronicle of Roger of Wendover

After twelve years of delays, Frederick II embarked from Italy in 1227, only to put back to port because plague had stricken his army. Pope Gregory IX, however, exasperated by Frederick's procrastination, summarily excommunicated the emperor. The crusade began without the emperor, but by 1228 Frederick, in spite of the ban of the Church, sailed for Cyprus and Jerusalem. His adventures were variously interpreted, favorably by some, very unfavorably by others. The following selections offer an alternation of views, two from chronicles, two from letters.

How a Great Stir Was Made at This Time to Assist in the Crusade, 1227

In the same year at the end of June, a great stir was made to aid the cross by all the crusaders throughout the world, who were so numerous, that from the kingdom of England alone forty thousand tried men were said to have marched, besides women and old men. This was declared by master Hubert, one of the preachers in England, who asserted that he had in fact set down as many as that in his roll. All these, and especially the poor, on whom the divine pleasure generally rests, entered upon the crusade with such devotion that they, without doubt, obtained favour with the Almighty, as was shown by manifest indications; for on the night of the nativity of St. John the Baptist, the Lord showed himself in the sky as when crucified; for on a most shining cross there appeared the body of our Lord pierced with nails and with a lance, and sprinkled with blood, so that the Saviour of the world by this showed his faithful followers in the world that he was appeased by the devotion of his people. This vision was seen by numbers, and amongst others by a trader, who was carrying fish for sale near the town of Uxbridge; being struck with astonishment at the strange apparition, and awed by the brightness of it, he was, as it were, lost in ecstasy and stood in amaze, not knowing what to do. His son, however, who was his only companion, comforted his father, and asked him to stop his cart and give praise to God for having conde-scended to show them such a vision. On the next day, and indeed every day after, wherever he exposed his fish for sale, he publicly told every one of the heavenly vision he had seen, and added his son's evidence to his own; many put faith in their story, but some disbelieved it, till they were induced to believe it by the number of visions which appeared about the same time to many in various places; and in these the cru-cified One himself deigned to open the heavens and to show to the incredulous his wonderful glory with immense splen-dour. Amongst others who went from England to join in the crusade were the bishops Peter, of Winchester, and William of Exeter, who had now fulfilled their vow of pilgrimage for nearly five years.

Of the Progress of the Crusade at This Time

How the business of the cross prospered in this crusade will plainly appear by the following letter which pope Gregory sent to all the faithful followers of Christ; "Gregory, bishop, servant of the servants of God, to all faithful Christians, greet-ing, &c. Be it known to the whole community of you that we have received letters from the country beyond sea to the following purport:—Gerald, by the divine mercy, patriarch of Jerusalem, P. archbishop of Caesarea, the humble and unworthy legate of the apostolic see, and N. archbishop of Narbonne, P. bishop of Winchester, and W. bishop of Exeter, the masters of the hospitallers, of the knights of the temple, and of the Teutonic order of hospitallers, to all to whom these letters may come, health in our Lord Jesus Christ. We are compelled to inform the whole community of you of our most urgent necessities, and of our progress in the cause of Jesus Christ, who shed his blood for all of the true faith. It is with much fervour of mind and shedding of tears, that his serene highness the emperor did not, as we all hoped, come into Syria in the month of August last past as he had promised. On this the pilgrims from those districts, hearing that the said emperor had not arrived in the aforesaid passage, amounting to more than forty thousand strong men, returned in the same ships as they had come, putting their trust in man rather than God. After their departure there remained here nearly eight hundred knights, who continued to cry with one consent, "Either let us break the truce or let us all depart together"; and they have been detained here not without great difficulty, because the duke of Limburg, a man of noble birth, has been appointed to command the army in the place of the emperor. A council was therefore held, especially of the hospitallers, templars, and of the German hospitallers, and it was agreed that the duke aforesaid should act as seemed most expedient for the cause of Christianity and the Holy Land; the duke then, having asked and received advice on these points, appeared on a day specially appointed for the purpose before us and some of the nobles of that country, and there openly declared that he wished to break the truce, and asked the assistance and advice of those present, as to how he could proceed most advantageously in that intention. And when the duke and his councellors were told that it would be dangerous to break the truce, and, as it was confirmed by oath, dishonourable as well, they replied that his holiness the pope had excommunicated all those crusaders who would not join in this crusade, although he knew that the truce was to continue for two years more; and by this they understood that he did not wish the truce to be kept, and, besides this, the pilgrims would not remain there idle. There were also many who said that, if the pilgrims were to go away, the Saracens would, after their departure, attack them, notwithstanding the truce. Some also thought

that Coradin was engaged in a fierce war with the rulers of
Haman, Camyle, and Aleppo, and on that account was more
than usually afraid of the truce being broken by the Christians; and if the truce were broken, they thought that Coradin, on seeing himself pressed by war on all sides, would
probably offer terms of peace. At length after a long discussion on these matters, all unanimously agreed to march to the
holy city, which Jesus Christ consecrated with his own blood;
and that the approach might be more easy, it was unanimously determined to fortify in the first place Caesarea, and
then Joppa, which they hoped undoubtedly to be able to do
before the passage of the ensuing August, and then they
would be able in the following winter to set out joyfully for
the house of the Lord, under his protection. This determination was made public outside the city of Acre on the feast of
the aspostles Simon and Jude, in the presence of all the pilgrims, and there they were solemnly enjoined to be ready on
the day after all Saints' day, to set out towards Caesarea; the
pilgrims, who did not know of the plan which the army had
determined on, on hearing this, after strengthening the
above-mentioned fortresses, were suddenly seized with such
a great desire to proceed to Jerusalem that they wept abun-
dantly, and they felt so strengthened by the grace of the Holy
Spirit, that each man felt as if he could overcome a thousand
enemies, and two could conquer ten thousand. We need not
therefore use many entreaties in urging it on you, when such
pressing necessity speaks for itself and demands immediate
assistance; for delay brings danger, and speed will be produc-
tive of the greatest advantages. The blood of Christ calls from
this country on each and every one; this small and humble,
though devout, army entreats for speedy assistance, hoping
and trusting in the Lord that this business, commenced in all
humility, may be by his favour brought to a happy termination. Do you therefore, each and all of you, exert yourselves
to assist the holy land, since this may be considered the common cause both of your faith and of the whole Christian
people. And we, under God's care and guidance, will not
cease to promote the cause, confidently hoping, that it may

prosper in the hands of the faithful who persevere with confidence. Given at the Lateran, the 23rd of December, in the first year of our pontificate."

How the Crusade Was Impeded through the Absence of the Emperor

In the mean time the emperor Frederick, who with other crusaders had, under penalty of excommunication by the pope in the before-mentioned passage, determined to fulfill his vow of pilgrimage, went to the Mediterranean sea, and embarked with a small retinue; but after pretending to make for the Holy Land for three days, he said that he was seized with a sudden illness, so that he could not at the risk of his life any longer endure the roughness of the sea and an unhealthy climate, therefore he altered his course, and after three days' sail landed at the port where he had embarked; and on this, the pilgrims from different parts of the world, who had preceded him to the Holy Land in hopes of having him as a leader and protector in fighting the enemies of the cross, were struck with consternation at hearing that the emperor had not come, as he had promised in the passage of August, and therefore, embarking in the ships in which they had sailed to the Holy Land, they returned home to the number of about forty thousand armed men; and this conduct of the emperor redounded much to his disgrace, and to the injury of the whole business of the crusade. It was on this account, in the opinion of many, that the Saviour of the world showed himself, as above related, to the Christians suspended on the cross, pierced with nails and sprinkled with blood, as if laying a complaint before each and every Christian, of the injury inflicted on him by the emperor.

How the Emperor Frederick Arrived at the Holy Land and Promoted the Cause of the Crusade, 1228

In the same year the Roman emperor, Frederick, took ship at the Mediterranean sea, and on the feast of the blessed virgin Mary, landed at Acre, where the clergy and people of that place came to meet him, and received him with the honours due to such a great man; but when they found out that he was excommunicated by the pope they did not confer on him the kiss of peace, nor did they sit at table with him, but they advised him to give satisfaction to the pope and return to the community of the holy church. The templars and hospitallers, however, on his arrival, went on their knees and worshipped him, kissing his knees; and the whole of the Christian army which was present there gave praise to God for his arrival, being now in hopes that by his means there would be salvation in Israel. The emperor then complained bitterly to the whole army against the Roman pontiff, that the latter had unjustly pronounced the sentence against him, asserting that he had delayed marching to the assistance of the Holy Land, on account of serious illness. The sultan of Babylon, when he heard of the emperor's arrival in Syria, sent him a number of costly presents of gold and silver, silks and jewels, camels and elephants, bears and monkeys, and other wonderful things which are not to be found in western countries. The emperor, on his arrival at Acre, found the Christian army under the command of the duke of Limburgh, the patriarach of Jerusalem, the archbishops of Nazareth, Caesarea, and Narbonne, the English bishops of Winchester and Exeter, the masters of the hospitallers, templars, and of the Teutonic order of hospitallers, who had under their joint command about eight hundred red pilgrim knights, and about ten thousand foot soldiers assembled from different parts of the world; and all these, inspired with a common feeling of devotion, marched to Caesarea, and had garrisoned some castles there, so that it now only remained for them to restore Joppa and then to march on the holy city. The emperor on learning the condition of the Holy Land, fully approved of the plan of the pilgrims, and, having made all necessary preparations to march forward, they set out preceded by the emperor, and on the 15th of November arrived without obstruction at Joppa. But as it was impossible for each man to carry by land provisions enough for himself and his horses for several days, as well as his baggage, ships had been procured at Acre for the purpose of bringing provisions to the army, but a sudden storm arose and the sea became so rough that for seven successive days the Christian pilgrims were without provisions. Great alarm then arose amongst many of them, that the Lord in his anger would destroy his people from the face of the earth; however, the unspeakable mercy of God, which allows no man to be tried beyond endurance, was at length aroused by the lamentations of his faithful people, and he commanded the winds and the sea and there was a calm; then a great number of ships arrived, under the guidance of the Lord, at Joppa, loaded with immense quantities of corn and barley, wine, and all kinds of provisions, so that there was always an abundant supply of provisions in the army till the said fortress was rebuilt.

How the Holy Land Was Restored to the Emperor Frederick, 1229

In the same year, our Lord Jesus Christ, the Saviour and Consoler of the world, visited his people in his compassion, and in compliance with the prayers of the universal church, restored to the Christian people in general, but to the Roman emperor Frederick in particular, the city of Jerusalem and the whole country which the Lord our Redeemer and Son of God had consecrated by his blood. Such was the good-will of our Lord to his people, of him who exalts the merciful to eternal life, that he may work vengeance on the nations, and dissension amongst the tribes of the Saracens. For at that time the sultan of Babylon was so severely harassed by internal wars in all directions, that not being able to attend to more, he was compelled to make a truce of ten years with the emperor, and to give up the Holy Land to the Christians without bloodshed. And thus a good war was sent by the Lord that a bad peace might be broken.

Of the Signs Preceding the Restoration of the Holy Land*

It should be remarked concerning this restoration of the land of promise and Jerusalem to the Christians, that as the astronomers of Toledo, before this cause of general rejoicing and exultation amongst Christians, wrote concerning the concourse of the planets, and of the dreadful storms of wind, so that they would stand together, and at the same time that there would be an earthquake, and an eclipse of the sun as well as the moon, which has been before mentioned amongst the events of this year, in the same way, before the taking of the Holy Land and the cross of our Lord by that perfidious and cruel man Saladin, some other astronomers then living in the same city also wrote to pope Clement as follows:— From the present year, which is the one thousand one hundred and seventy-ninth year of our Lord's incarnation, till the expiration of seven years, in the month of September, the sun being in Libra and the tail of the Dragon, there will be, if God so permit, an assembling of the planets in Libra and the tail of the Dragon, and this is a wonderful signification of a change of immutable events. And there shall follow a dreadful earthquake, and the accustomed places of perdition shall be destroyed by Saturn and Mars, &c. This conjunction of the planets will produce a strong wind, which will thicken and darken the air, and infect it with poison, and the sound of this wind will be dreadful, disturbing the hearts of men; and from sandy regions it shall raise the sand and overwhelm the cities lying nearest to them in the plains, and in the first place the eastern cities of Mecca and Babylon, and all cities lying near to sandy places; not one will escape being over-

*These two chapters are omitted in Paris, instead of which is a description of the great seal attached to the emperor's bull. "The form of the emperor's golden bull was as follows:—On one side was the royal figure, and around it was written, 'Frederick, by the grace of God, the august emperor of the Romans.' On the same side as the royal figure, over the left shoulder, was written, 'King of Jerusalem'; in another part, over the left shoulder, were the words, 'King of Sicily.' On the other side of the bull was engraved a city, representing Rome, and around it was written, 'Rome, the head of the world, holds the reigns of the round world.' This bull was somewhat larger than the pope's."

whelmed with sand and earth. But signs of these events will precede them; in the same year there will be, before the planets assemble in Libra, a total eclipse of the sun, and in the preceding conflict the moon will be totally eclipsed; and the eclipse of the sun will be of a fiery and unsightly colour, denoting that there will be a war amongst chiefs near a river in the east, and likewise in western countries; and a doubtfulness shall fall amongst the Jews and Saracens, until they shall altogether abandon their synagogues and mosques, and their sect shall at the command of God be entirely destroyed and annihilated; wherefore, when you see the eclipse, know that you are to leave that land with all your followers.

How on Account of the Sins of Man the Holy Land Was Lost

At that time there was much evil amongst men on earth, so that "all flesh almost had corrupted its way before the Lord;" for the practice of sin had burst forth amonst the people to such a degree, that all, casting aside the veil of shame, everywhere inclined to wickedness openly. Too tedious is it to enumerate the slaughters, robberies, adultery, obscenities, lies, treasons, and other crimes, especially so to us, who design to write of the events which occurred. However the old enemy of man after having disseminated the spirt of corruption far and wide in the world, invaded Syria in particular, from which place other nations received their religion in the first place, and from that place they then took the example of all uncleanness. For this reason therefore the Lord and Saviour of the world, seeing that the land of his nativity, suffering, and resurrection had fallen into the depths of wickedness, scorned his inheritance, and allowed the rod of his anger, namely Saladin, to vent his rage to the extermination of that obstinate race; for he preferred that the Holy Land should for a short time be a slave to the profane rites of nations, than that those people should any longer flourish, who were not restrained from unlawful actions by any regard to probity. The approach of the destruction which was to happen, was prognosticated by divers events, namely by a great famine, frequent earthquakes, and eclipses of the sun and moon; but the storm of wind, which the astronomers of Toledo, from an inspection of the stars, had pronounced would come from the assembling of the planets, together with a mortality and foul atmosphere, was without doubt changed to signify this event; for in the spring there was a heavy wind which shook the four quarters of the world, and signified that its different nations would be stirred up to battle and to the destruction of the Holy Land. And the holy city of Jerusalem, with the whole land of promise, and also the life-giving cross of our Lord, remained in the hands of the enemies of Christ for forty-two years up to this present year, which is the one thousand two hundred and twenty-ninth year of our Lord's incarnation, when at length the time arrived for our Lord in his compassion to give heed to the prayers of his humble servants, and to rebuild Sion, to appear in his glory in the place of his holy nativity, suffering, and resurrection, to hear the lamentations of his enslaved people, and to release the sons of the destroyed ones. Truly and without doubt did the Lord hear the groans of his enslaved people at the restoration of the Holy Land, which at that time was brought about by the diligence of the emperor Frederick, with the co-operation of the divine clemency, inasmuch as all the captives who were in the power of the pagans and subjected to the vilest kinds of slavery, were now released from the yoke of bondage and came to the holy city of Jerusalem, where they showed themselves to many and after having paid their devotions in the sacred places of the holy city, returned to their own countries in various parts of the world, praising and blessing God in all things, for they had heard and seen what wonderful works the Lord had done for them and showed to them.

Of the Reconciliation of the Holy City of Jerusalem and Other Places

The army of the Christians then, as we have said, entered the holy city of Jerusalem, and the patriarch, with the suffragan bishops, purified the temple of the Lord and the church of his holy sepulchre and resurrection, and all the other sacred churches of the city; they washed the pavement and walls with holy water, and forming processions with hymns and psalms they reconciled to God all his places which had been so long defiled by the filth of the pagans, but as long as the emperor, who was excommunicated, remained inside the city, no prelate dared to perform mass in it. However a certain master Walter, a religious, wise, and discreet man, of the order of preachers, who had been entrusted by the pope with the duty of preaching in the army of Christ, which duty he had for a long time prosperously fulfilled, performed divine services in the suburban churches, by which he greatly excited the devotion of the Christians. After then the prelates, inferior as well as superior, and all the religious men had had their churches and old possessions restored to them, and had rejoiced in all the heavenly gifts which had been bestowed on them far beyond their expectations, they all set to work in conjunction with the rest of the pilgrims, at great expense and trouble, to rebuild the city, to surround the walls with trenches, and to repair the ramparts of the towers; and not only was this done in the holy city of Jerusalem, but also in all the cities and fortresses of that land, which Jesus Christ had trodden with his holy feet, and consecrated with his sacred blood.

2. The Crusade of Frederick II: From the History of Philip of Novara

Philip, in the service of the powerful Syrian-Frankish family of the Ibelins, Lords of Beirut, was extremely hostile to Frederick, not so much for Frederick's high-handed treatment of his crusader's vow as for his high-handed treatment of the Lords of Ibelin and the King of Jerusalem, John of Brienne. The description is in marked contrast to that of Roger of Wendover. The translation printed here is taken from John L. LaMonte, The Wars of Frederick II against the Ibelins in Syria and Cyprus *by Philip de Novare, Records of*

Civilization, Sources and Studies, Number 25 (New York: Columbia University Press, 1936), pp. 87–93. Reprinted with permission.

In the year 1229 [1228] the emperor came to Syria with all his navy and the king and all his Cypriots with him. The lord of Beirut went to Beirut and was most gladly beheld there, for no lord was ever more dearly loved by his men. He remained only one day, and then at once followed the emperor and joined him at Tyre. The emperor was very well received in Syria and all did homage to him. He left Tyre and went to the city of Acre, and was received there with honor.[1] His fleet, which consisted of seventy galleys and ships, entered the port of Acre, and he [the emperor] was quartered in the castle. Then he had the liegemen assembled and demanded of them that they do homage to him[2] as the bailli because he had a small son who was called King Conrad and was rightful heir to the kingdom of Jerusalem through his mother who was dead. The emperor, his men, and all the men of Syria left Acre to go to Jaffa, and there they made terms of truce with El Kamel,[3] who was then sultan of Babylon and Damascus[4]

1. The papal excommunication, which was published in Syria shortly after Frederick's arrival, estranged the clergy and the Templars and Hospitallers, though the Teutonic Knights stood by the emperor and the Syrian barons paid little attention to it.

2. This passage, beginning "He left Tyre . . .," might seem to indicate that Frederick stopped first at Tyre and then went on to Acre, and the fact that John d'Ibelin joined him at Tyre after stopping first at Beirut would confirm this impression.

3. El Malik el Kamel abou'l Mealy Mohammed ibn Abou Bekr ben Ayyoub (1218-38), eldest son of Sayf al Din and nephew of Saladin, was the ruler of Egypt after the death of his father.

4. Babylon of course refers to Egypt. It is not true that El Kamel was at this time sultan of Damascus. El Moadden Isa, a younger brother of El Kamel, ruled Damascus 1218-27, and was succeeded by his son El Malik en Nasir Daoud. At first Daoud was able to enter into his inheritance with the approval of his other uncle, El Aschraf Musa of Mesopotamia, but in 1228 El Kamel and El Aschraf entered into an alliance to divide the territories of Damascus. By this alliance El Kamel received Palestine while El Aschraf got Damascus and the northern parts of El Moadden's posessions. The siege of Damascus by El Aschraf was going on all the time that Frederick was in Palestine, and the desire to be free to take part therein was one of the reasons that El Kamel granted the favorable treaty he did.

and who held Jerusalem and all the country; thereby were surrendered Jerusalem and Nazareth and Lydda to the emperor.

In the same year [1229], in the midst of all these events, the emperor sent Count Stephen of Botron[5] to Cyprus, and other Longobards as well, and had all the fortresses and revenues of the crown seized for his use, and he said that he was the bailli and that it was his right. The Cypriots were much afeared as were their women and children, and they placed themselves in the charge of the clergy wherever they were able. Some fled outside of Cyprus; notably Sir John d'Ibelin[6] —who later became count of Jaffa and who was at that time a child—with his sister and other gentlefolk fled in the heart of winter, and they encountered such bad weather that they barely escaped drowning; however with the aid of God they reached Tortosa. The emperor held Cyprus; the Cypriots who were in his host were very ill at ease and, if the lord of Beirut would have consented to it, they would have carried off and kidnapped young King Henry and would have deserted the emperor.

The emperor was by now unpopular with all the people of Acre, especially was he disliked by the Templars;[7] and at that time there was a most valiant brother of the Temple, Brother

5. This should be Cotron not Botron. This is Stephen, count of Cotron, whom Frederick sent to Syria in 1225 with three hundred knights from Sicily to accompany the bishop of Melfi and receive the homages of the Jerusalemite barons on the occasion of the marriage of the emperor and the queen of Jerusalem.

6. John d'Ibelin of Jaffa, son of Philip d'Ibelin, was later to become the patron and pupil of Philip de Novare. He is the author of the great work on the Assizes of Jerusalem. As he was seventeen in 1232, he must have been fifteen at this time.

7. Both the Templars and Hospitallers refused to follow Frederick as he was excommunicate and under the ban of the papacy. They finally agreed to coöperate with his army as allies serving under the "ban of Christ" and not under the command of the emperor. Frederick attempted in vain to get possession of the Templars' castle of Chateau Pelerin and accused the Templars of attempting to assassinate him. The Teutonic Knights served the emperor willingly and were loyal to him throughout, but the other Orders respected the papal commands and refused to obey the emperor. The opposition of the Orders and of the patriarch is told of in the letters of Gerold, Herman, et al., and Ryccardus S. Germano.

Peter de Montaigu,[8] who was very brave and noble; and most valiant and wise was also the master of the Teutonic Knights;[9] and the people of the plain[10] were not well inclined towards the emperor. The emperor did much that seemed evil, and he always kept galleys under arms, with their oars in the locks, even in winter. Many men said that he wished to capture the lord of Beirut, his children, Sir Anceau de Brie, and others of his friends, the master of the Temple and other people, and that he wished to send them to Apulia. On one occasion they said that he wished to kill them at a council to which he had called and summoned them, but they became aware of it and came in such strength that he did not dare to do it. However he made his truce with the Saracens as was desired and went to Jerusalem,[11] and thereafter came to Acre. The lord of Beirut never left him and, though there were those who often advised him to leave, he did not wish to do it.

At Acre the emperor assembled his men and had all the people of the city come there, and there were many Pisans who were very well disposed toward him. He addressed them and stated that which he desired; and in his address he complained much of the Temple.

He laid siege to the house of the Temple;[12] and the house

8. Peter de Montaigu, grand master 1219-32, brother of Archbishop Eustorgue of Nicosia.

9. Herman von Salza, grand master 1210-39, was one of Frederick's most trusted advisers. It was he who helped negotiate the marriage with the queen of Jerusalem securing for Frederick the throne of Jerusalem. He is best known for procuring for the Knights the privileges in Prussia which later formed the basis for their territorial state.

10. The "people of the plain" probably refers to the population of the coastal plain around Acre.

11. This is Novare's only mention of Frederick's coronation in Jerusalem on March 18, 1229. The *Eracles* (p. 374) gives the account of the coronation from the Syrian point of view, noting that the Cypriot contingent remained at Jaffa and did not accompany the emperor to the Holy City. This circumstance may account for the omission of any mention of the coronation by Novare. The Ibelin faction could not recognize this coronation as they recognized Frederick only as bailli for Conrad, the legitimate heir.

12. The siege lasted five days according to Gerold. A letter of Gerold of May, 1229, complains that Frederick besieged him in his patriarchal palace. Kantorowicz, *Frederick II* (pp. 204-5) claims that the people were incited by

of the Temple was badly damaged, for the convent was all outside, but thereupon many folk came to it both by sea and by land. I do not know how long the siege lasted, but villainously he abandoned it.[13] The emperor arranged for his passage secretly, and on the first day of May at dawn, without letting it be known by anyone, he got into a galley before the street of the butchers. Whence it happened that the butchers and the old people of the street, who were most ill disposed, ran along beside him and pelted him with tripe and bits of meat most scurrilously.

The lord of Beirut and Sir Eudes de Montbéliard[14] heard talk of this; and they hurried there and drove away with blows those who had been throwing things at him, and they cried to him from the land to where he was on the galley that they commended him to God. The emperor replied in so low a voice that I do not know whether it was well or ill; he said that he was leaving as baillies in his place the lord of Sidon and Garnier l'Aleman.[15] The emperor had very

the patriarch against Frederick. Frederick's enmity toward the Temple continued after his return to Italy, and he confiscated all its lands in his domains.

13. The Templars, Genoese, and John of Beirut formed a working alliance against the emperor and protected themselves.

14. Eudes de Montbéliard, constable of Jerusalem 1218-44, had been appointed bailli of Jerusalem by King John de Brienne in 1223 and had been continued in that office by Frederick at the time of his marriage. In July, 1227, he was replaced by Count Thomas of Acerra but on the death of Isabelle was elected as bailli for Conrad by the barons, with Balian of Sidon as his colleague. These two were in possession of the bailliage when the emperor arrived in Acre. Eudes returned to the bailliage when Garnier l'Aleman resigned to become a Templar in 1239 and again when Conrad became of age in 1243. He favored the rights of King Conrad against the Ibelins although he was closely related to that house: he was the son of Walter de Montbéliard and Borgogne de Lusignan, his aunt Alice was the wife of Philip d'Ibelin, his sister Eschive married Balian the son of John of Beirut, he himself married Eschive de Tiberias, the granddaughter of Helvis d'Ibelin and niece of Balian of Sidon. His daughter married Philip d'Ibelin the son of Baldwin.

15. Garnier l'Aleman has been identified by E. Winkelmann as Werner von Egisheim, an Alsatian. He was one of the earlier members of his house in the East and contributed to its rise to importance. He married Pavie de Gibelet, and their son John became lord of Caesarea through marriage. His family was imperialist in sentiment and his nephew Garnier the younger was a member of the imperialist-Cypriot colony in Corfu under Philip Chenart. The *Eracles* (p. 388) gives Aymon de Laron as chatelain of Tyre, and

well equipped the castle of Tyre, and he gave it to the lord of Sidon to command and made it appear that he trusted much in him; but King Henry of Cyprus he took with him.

Thus the emperor left Acre; hated, cursed, and vilified. He arrived in Cyprus at Limassol, and there established the aforementioned King Henry and gave him to wife one of his cousins, the daughter of the Marquis of Montferrat.[16] There he made the final terms with the five baillies, whom you have heard named already, who were of his party, selling them the bailliage of Cyprus and of the land for ten thousand marks, until the majority of the aforesaid king of Cyprus.[17] He had them swear that they would not suffer the lord of Beirut and his partisans to return to Cyprus, and he commanded that they should dispossess them. They accepted this willingly from the emperor, whereat he turned over to them mercenaries, German, Flemish, and Longobard, whom they themselves should pay, and they sought and hired mercenaries in Acre and in other places. Certain men of the king, because of the fact that they [the baillies] had King Henry with them and moved by desire to return to their homes, joined with them and placed themselves under their command; but the castles were not surrendered to them until they had paid the money. The emperor Frederick went on over the sea and left in his place men to receive the money and deliver to them the castles.[18]

Röhricht cites no authority for this amazing statement which was certainly not consistent with Frederick's policy towards the Ibelins.

16. Alice de Montferrat, daughter of William IV de Montferrat and Bertha of Gravesane, was cousin of neither Frederick nor Henry, her relationship to Henry being that she was great-niece of Conrad, the husband of Isabelle of Jerusalem. William III of Montferrat was the common great-grandfather of Alice and of Isabelle, Frederick's deceased wife, and his wife Sophia was the daughter of Frederick I and aunt of Frederick II.

17. Frederick had sold the bailliage to Amaury Barlais and his four companions before he left Acre. At Limassol the agreement was renewed. The bailliage was for three years.

18. The *Eracles* says: "And he told them that they should render the ten thousand marks to Balian of Sidon and Garnier l'Aleman who were remaining in his place as baillies of Jerusalem."

3. Letter from Frederick II to Henry III of England, 1229: The Imperial Achievement

Frederick was his own best propagandist, and his account of his crusading triumphs stands in sharp contrast to the next selection. His own account is from Roger of Wendover.

Frederick, by the grace of God, the august emperor of the Romans, king of Jerusalem and Sicily, to his well-beloved friend Henry, king of the English, health and sincere affection.

Let all rejoice and exult in the Lord, and let those who are correct in heart glorify Him, who, to make known His power, does not make boast of horses and chariots, but has now gained glory for Himself, in the scarcity of His soldiers, that all may know and understand that He is glorious in His majesty, terrible in His magnificence, and wonderful in His plans on the sons of men, changing seasons at will, and bringing the hearts of different nations together; for in these few days, by a miracle rather than by strength, that business has been brought to a conclusion, which for a length of time past many chiefs and rulers of the world amongst the multitude of nations, have never been able till now to accomplish by force, however great, nor by fear.

Not, therefore, to keep you in suspense by a long account, we wish to inform your holiness, that we, firmly putting our trust in God, and believing that Jesus Christ, His Son, in whose service we have so devotedly exposed our bodies and lives, would not abandon us in these unknown and distant countries, but would at least give us wholesome advice and assistance for His honor, praise, and glory, boldly in the name set forth from Acre on the fifteenth day of the month of November last past and arrived safely at Joppa, intending to rebuild the castle at that place with proper strength, that afterwards the approach to the holy city of Jerusalem might be not only easier, but also shorter and more safe for us as well as for all Christians. When, therefore, we were, in the confidence of our trust in God, engaged at Joppa, and superintending the building of the castle and the cause of Christ, as necessity required and as was our duty, and whilst all our pilgrims were busily engaged in these matters, several messengers often passed to and fro between us and the sultan of Babylon; for he and another sultan, called Xaphat, his brother, were with a large army at the city of Gaza, distant about one day's journey from us; in another direction, in the city of Sichen, which is commonly called Neapolis, and situated in the plains, the sultan of Damascus, his nephew, was staying with an immense number of knights and soldiers also about a day's journey from us and the Christians.

And whilst the treaty was in progress between the parties on either side of the restoration of the Holy Land, at length Jesus Christ, the Son of God, beholding from on high our devoted endurance and patient devotion to His cause, in His merciful compassion of us, at length brought it about that the sultan of Babylon restored to us the holy city, the place where the feet of Christ trod,[1] and where the true worshippers adore the Father in spirit and in truth. But that we may inform you of the particulars of this surrender each as they happened, be it known to you that not only is the body of the aforesaid city restored to us, but also the whole of the country extending from thence to the sea-coast near the castle of Joppa, so that for the future pilgrims will have free passage and a safe return to and from the sepulchre; provided, however, that the Saracens of that part of the country, since they hold the temple in great veneration, may come there as often as they choose in the character of pilgrims, to worship according to their custom, and that we shall henceforth permit them to come, however, only as many as we may choose to allow, and without arms, nor are they to dwell in the city, but outside, and as soon as they have paid their devotions they are to depart.

Moreover, the city of Bethlehem is restored to us, and all the country between Jerusalem and that city; as also the city of Nazareth, and all the country between Acre and that city; the whole of the district of Turon, which is very extensive,

1. This is in Psalm 132. The English version is "Before thy footstool." The translation in the letter is from the Vulgate and is due to a mistake made by St. Jerome.

and very advantageous to the Christians; the city of Sidon, too, is given up to us with the whole plain and its appurtenances, which will be the more acceptable to the Christians the more advantageous it has till now appeared to be to the Saracens, especially as there is a good harbor there, and from there great quantities of arms and necessaries might be carried to the city of Damascus, and often from Damascus to Babylon. And although according to our treaty we are allowed to rebuild the city of Jerusalem in as good a state as it has ever been, and also the castles of Joppa, Cesarea, Sidon, and that of St. Mary of the Teutonic order, which the brothers of that order have begun to build in the mountainous district of Acre, and which it has never been allowed the Christians to do during any former truce; nevertheless the sultan is not allowed, till the end of the truce between him and us, which is agreed on for ten years, to repair or rebuild any fortresses or castles.

And so on Sunday, the eighteenth day of February last past, which is the day on which Christ, the Son of God, rose from the dead, and which, in memory of His resurrection, is solemnly cherished and kept holy by all Christians in general throughout the world, this treaty of peace was confirmed by oath between us. Truly then on us and on all does that day seem to have shone favorably, in which the angels sing in praise of God, "Glory to God on high, and on earth peace, and good-will toward men." And in acknowledgment of such great kindness and of such an honor, which, beyond our deserts and contrary to the opinion of many, God has mercifully conferred on us, to the lasting renown of His compassion, and that in His holy place we might personally offer to Him the burnt offering of our lips, be it known to you that on the seventeenth day of the month of March of this second indiction, we, in company with all the pilgrims who had with us faithfully followed Christ, the Son of God, entered the holy city of Jerusalem, and after worshipping at the holy sepulchre, we, as being a Catholic emperor, on the following day, wore the crown, which Almighty God provided for us from the throne of His majesty, when of His especial grace, He exalted us on high amongst the princes of the world; so that whilst we have supported the honor of this high dignity, which belongs to us by right of sovereignty, it is more and more evident to all that the hand of the Lord hath done all this; and since His mercies are over all His works, let the worshippers of the orthodox faith henceforth know and relate it far and wide throughout the world, that He, who is blessed for ever, has visited and redeemed His people, and has raised up the horn of salvation for us in the house of His servant David.

And before we leave the city of Jerusalem, we have determined magnificently to rebuild it, and its towers and walls, and we intend so to arrange matters that, during our absence, there shall be no less care and diligence used in the business, than if we were present in person. In order that this our present letter may be full of exultation throughout, and so a happy end correspond with its happy beginning, and rejoice your royal mind, we wish it be known to our ally, that the said sultan is bound to restore to us all those captives whom he did not in accordance with the treaty made between him and the Christians deliver up at the time when he lost Damietta some time since, and also the others who have been since taken.

Given at the holy city of Jerusalem, on the seventeenth day of the month of March, in the year of our Lord one thousand two hundred and twenty-nine.

4. Letter from Gerold, Patriarch of Jerusalem, to the Christian Faithful: The Coming of Antichrist

The following selection is from the Chronicle of Matthew Paris. Translation D. C. Munro, Letters of the Crusaders, *University of Pennsylvania Translations and Reprints from the Original Sources of European History, Vol. I, no. 4 (Philadelphia, 1896), pp. 25-29.*

Gerold, patriarch of Jerusalem, to all the faithful—greeting.

If it should be fully known how astonishing, nay rather,

deplorable, the conduct of the emperor has been in the eastern lands from beginning to end, to the great detriment of the cause of Jesus Christ and to the great injury of the Christian faith, from the sole of his foot to the top of his head no common sense would be found in him. For he came, excommunicated, without money and followed by scarcely forty knights, and hoped to maintain himself by spoiling the inhabitants of Syria. He first came to Cyprus and there most discourteously seized that nobleman J. [John] of Ibelin and his sons, whom he had invited to his table under pretext of speaking of the affairs of the Holy Land. Next the king, whom he had invited to meet him, he retained almost as a captive. He thus by violence and fraud got possession of the kingdom.

After these achievements he passed over into Syria. Although in the beginning he promised to do marvels, and although in the presence of the foolish he boasted loudly, he immediately sent to the sultan of Babylon to demand peace. This conduct rendered him despicable in the eyes of the sultan and his subjects, especially after they had discovered that he was not at the head of a numerous army, which might have to some extent added weight to his words. Under the pretext of defending Joppa, he marched with the Christian army towards that city, in order to be nearer the sultan and in order to be able more easily to treat of peace or obtain a truce. What more shall I say? After long and mysterious conferences, and without having consulted any one who lived in the country, he suddenly announced one day that he had made peace with the sultan. No one saw the text of the peace or truce when the emperor took the oath to observe the articles which were agreed upon. Moreover, you will be able to see clearly how great the malice was and how fraudulent the tenor of certain articles of the truce which we have decided to send to you. The emperor, for giving credit to his word, wished as a guarantee only the word of the sultan, which he obtained. For he said, among other things, that the holy city was surrendered to him.

He went thither with the Christian army on the eve of the Sunday when *"Oculi mei"* is sung [third Sunday in Lent]. The Sunday following, without any fitting ceremony and although excommunicated, in the chapel of the sepulchre of our Lord, to the manifest prejudice of his honor and of the imperial dignity, he put the diadem upon his forehead, although the Saracens still held the temple of the Lord and Solomon's temple, and although they proclaimed publicly as before the law of Mohammed—to the great confusion and chagrin of the pilgrims.

This same prince, who had previously very often promised to fortify Jerusalem, departed in secrecy from the city at dawn on the following Monday. The Hospitalers and the Templars promised solemnly and earnestly to aid him with all their forces and their advice, if he wanted to fortify the city, as he had promised. But the emperor, who did not care to set affairs right, and who saw that there was no certainty in what had been done, and that the city in the state in which it had been surrendered to him could be neither defended nor fortified, was content with the name of surrender, and on the same day hastened with his family to Joppa. The pilgrims who had entered Jerusalem with the emperor, witnessing his departure, were unwilling to remain behind.

The following Sunday when *"Laetare Jerusalem"* is sung [fourth Sunday in Lent], he arrived at Acre. There in order to seduce the people and to obtain their favor, he granted them a certain privilege. God knows the motive which made him act thus, and his subsequent conduct will make it known. As, moreover, the passage was near, and as all pilgrims, humble and great, after having visited the Holy Sepulchre, were preparing to withdraw, as if they had accomplished their pilgrimage, because no truce had been concluded with the sultan of Damascus, we, seeing that the holy land was already deserted and abandoned by the pilgrims, in our council formed the plan of retaining soldiers, for the common good, by means of the alms given by the king of France of holy memory.

When the emperor heard of this, he said to us that he was astonished at this, since he had concluded a truce with the sultan of Babylon. We replied to him that the knife was still in the wound, since there was not a truce or peace with the sultan of Damascus, newphew of the aforesaid sultan and opposed to him, adding that even if the sultan of Babylon was unwilling, the former could still do us much harm. The emperor replied, saying that no soldiers ought to be retained in his kingdom without his advice and consent, as he was now king of Jerusalem. We answered to that, that in the matter in question, as well as in all of a similar nature, we were very sorry not to be able, without endangering the salvation of our souls, to obey his wishes, because he was excommunicated. The emperor made no response to us, but on the following day he caused the pilgrims who inhabited the city to be assembled outside by the public crier, and by special messengers he also convoked the prelates and the monks.

Addressing them in person, he began to complain bitterly of us, by heaping up false accusations. Then turning his remarks to the venerable master of the Templars he publicly attempted to severely tarnish the reputation of the latter, by various vain speeches, seeking thus to throw upon others the responsibility for his own faults which were now manifest, and adding at last, that we were maintaining troops with the purpose of injuring him. After that he ordered all foreign soldiers, of all nations, if they valued their lives and property, not to remain in the land from that day on, and ordered count Thomas, whom he intended to leave as bailiff of the country, to punish with stripes any one who was found lingering, in order that the punishment of one might serve as an example to many. After doing all this he withdrew, and would listen to no excuse or answers to the charges which he had so shamefully made. He determined immediately to post some cross-bowmen at the gates of the city, ordering them to allow the Templars to go out but not to return. Next he fortified with cross-bows the churches and other elevated positions, and especially those which commanded the communications between the Templars and ourselves. And you may be sure that he never showed as much animosity and hatred against Saracens.

For our part, seeing his manifest wickedness, we assembled all the prelates and all the pilgrims, and menaced with excommunication all those who should aid the emperor with their advice or their services against the Church, the Templars, the other monks of the holy land, or the pilgrims. The emperor was more and more irritated, and immediately caused all the passages to be guarded more strictly, refused to allow any kind of provisions to be brought to us or to the members of our party, and placed everywhere crossbowmen and archers, who attacked severely us, the Templars and the pilgrims. Finally to fill the measure of his malice, he caused some Dominicans and Minorites who had come on Palm Sunday to the proper places to announce the Word of God, to be torn from the pulpit, to be thrown down and dragged along the ground and whipped throughout the city, as if they had been robbers. Then seeing that he did not obtain what he had hoped from the above-mentioned siege, he treated of peace. We replied to him that we would not hear of peace until he sent away the cross-bowmen and other troops, until he had returned our property to us, until finally he had restored all things to the condition and freedom in which they were on that day when he entered Jerusalem. He finally ordered what we wanted to be done, but it was not executed. Therefore we placed the city under interdict.

The emperor, realizing that his wickedness could have no success, was unwilling to remain any longer in the country. And, as if he would have liked to ruin everything, he ordered the crossbows and engines of war, which for a long time had been kept at Acre for the defense of the Holy Land, to be secretly carried onto his vessels. He also sent away several of them to the sultan of Babylon, as his dear friend. He sent a troop of soldiers to Cyprus to levy heavy contributions of money there, and, what appeared to us more astonishing, he destroyed the galleys which he was not able to take with him. Having learned this, we resolved to reproach him with it, but shunning the remonstrance and the correction, he entered a galley secretly, by an obscure way, on the day of the Apostles St. Philip and St. James, and hastened to reach the island of Cyprus, without saying adieu to any one, leaving Joppa destitute; and may he never return!

Very soon the bailiffs of the above-mentioned sultan shut off all departure from Jerusalem for the Christian poor and the Syrians, and many pilgrims died thus on the road.

This is what the emperor did, to the detriment of the Holy Land and of his own soul, as well as many other things which are known and which we leave to others to relate. May the merciful God deign to soften the results! Farewell.